REALITY
THE HOPE OF GLORY

by Arthur Katz
with Philip Chomak

LOGOS INTERNATIONAL
PLAINFIELD, NEW JERSEY 07061

Also by Arthur Katz
Ben Israel

Selections on pp. 93, 94, 95 reprinted with permission of Farrar, Straus & Giroux, Inc. from NIGHT by Elie Wiesel. English translation Copyright © 1960 by MacGibbon & Kee. Originally published in French by Les Editions de Minuit, Copyright © 1958.

All direct Scripture quotations are from the King James Version, unless otherwise indicated.

REALITY

THE HOPE OF GLORY

FOREWORD

Sitting in my living room in the spring of 1974, listening to a little cassette tape recorder, I heard Art Katz's Brooklyn accent for the first time. The words that he spoke, telling of the necessity of brokenness and humility in the believer's life, were marked by the reality that can only come from the Spirit of Truth. That man's God was, I knew, my God. A few months later, I met Art during one of his visits to California; our bond of brotherhood in the Messiah Jesus was affirmed, and the seeds of our collaboration on this book were sown.

The four sections of *Reality* are based upon talks that Art has given both here and abroad. These messages to the body of Christ are not works of formal theology; they were born out of the experiences of a man who has prayerfully sought to deliver the living word of the Lord to God's people in the power of the Holy Spirit.

You will find no new theories, no special techniques, and no quick and easy steps to bliss in these pages. You *will* be pointed towards our Lord "in whom are hid all the treasures of wisdom and knowledge" (Colossians 2:3).

May He richly bless you as you walk in the Way.

Philip Chomak
Berkeley, California

PREFACE

If there can be said to be an attribute of life and character that is distinctly Jewish, perhaps it is a passion for reality and truth. Whatever the distortions and deflections in my own life till Christ, it has been and remains my single greatest preoccupation. Indeed, it brought me to Him who is Truth and continues by His grace unabated still in His service.

Smitten from the earliest believing by the apostolic grandeur of the Scriptures, I am with others impatient of any other standard, especially that which will characterize this final generation. This age, I believe, will conclude as it began—in ultimate collision between kingdoms, in ultimate controversy, contention, conflict and glory: All that is sham and pretense, all that is ungodly and unreal will dissipate when He will be seen finally in the glory of His people. It is my prayer that these messages of men committed to that vision will encourage others who love truth to persevere in hope of that same glory.

Dominion, Arthur Katz
Laporte, Minnesota 56461

Contents

REALITY

THE HOPE OF GLORY

Chapter One

But He Refused: Joseph and the End Times

Submit yourselves therefore to God.
Resist the devil, and he will flee from you.

James 4:7

The Revelation of True Jewishness

It is very strange that, after thirty-five years of being a Jew, I had virtually no real knowledge of the great patriarchal figures of Jewish life. Abraham, Isaac, Jacob, and Joseph were only names. There is no enigma greater in the life of a Jew than the enigma of his own Jewishness. It's a bewildering phenomenon with which most of us Jews have had to live. The best that we have been able to do in recent times has been to measure Jewishness by the amount of pastrami we consume, or by other innumerable manifestations of *Yiddishkeit* (the outward, ceremonial and cultural modes of my people). It is not until we are born of the Spirit of the Living God (*Ruach Hakodesh*) that we can begin to understand the true meaning of our own Jewishness; then God begins to open to us a very rich heritage indeed.

The Dreamer

We have been given something very rich in the life and character of Joseph. He was a rather strange one who was a dreamer, a type very familiar to Jewish life in general, and to myself in particular. I have been a dreamer, visionary, and idealist since the dawn of my adolescence, at around the time of my bar mitzvah.

At the age of twelve or thirteen, I was a troubled and perplexed kid; already out of joint with the world and its spirit; already an atheist; already consumed by a passion for truth and for understanding and finding neither; already realizing that the schools and all the paraphernalia of modern society had little to do or to say to remedy the obvious sickness of our human condition. Everything was compounded by the fact that, being born in 1929, I grew up in the Depression years, viewed terrible want and inequities, and approached young manhood during the

2

turbulence of World War II. To complete the picture, I was fed on the statistics of six million Jews who were murdered by the Nazi regime. If that's not enough to give anybody anguish of soul, I don't know what is.

Like all dreamer-visionary-idealists, I had an urgent sense and intuition that there must be a "reality" that lies beneath the confused, painful surface of things. I frantically pursued an unnamed "something" for thirty-five years, until I finally understood that it was I who was being chased by Someone named *Yeshua Hamasheach*. I received Him as the Lord and Savior of my then-broken life, and I was brought into fellowship with God. With His Spirit within me, I could put my own dreams and visions aside, and live for the revelation and fulfillment of His.

Living Accusations

As a dreamer and a visionary, Joseph was despised by his brothers. I believe that this will always be the case with such men, because they will not become one of the boys. He was despised not only for his dreams, but for the words that he spoke (Genesis 37:8). This relationship between Joseph and his brothers has a particular resonance which triggers something in my soul and gives me a suggestion of the kind of posture that the Josephs of this world are going to confront at the end of the ages. We, of all men, are going to be despised for our dreams and for the words that we shall speak. We are going to be conspicuously different from our brothers. We are going to look, sound, appear and *be* different.

Shortly after salvation in Jerusalem, I found myself back in California, reinstated as a teacher in the Oakland Public School system. I lived in a kind of confusion and perplexity, not having a mature understanding, wondering why the Living God, against Whom I had been a lifelong blasphemer

3

and enemy, would lovingly bring me into His Kingdom. On my first night back in the area, after sharing the gospel of Christ, I lost all my friends, except for one who later found himself, face down on his living room floor, giving his life to Jesus.

I remember sitting at a cafeteria table in the faculty dining room. There was a Jewish woman on that staff to whom, day after day, I was giving no peace. My ignorance about the things of God was great, but I was intent upon sharing what little I had. (If you use the one talent He has given you, God adds the more.) I used to come to that woman time and time again with my one or two Scriptures, the details of the experience of my profound conversion, or whatever I had, but on one occasion, I was completely silent. I don't know why. I just had absolutely nothing to say; my mouth was stopped. I was bent over, eating my lunch quietly, and I saw that she was growing increasingly irritated by my silence. Finally, after a continual mounting of pressure, she could not contain herself any longer, and blurted out, "Art, even when you're silent, you're a living accusation!"

I have never forgotten that statement, because I believe with all my heart that, as we press deeper into the end times, we are going to become accusations for the age, we Josephs of this generation, we dreamers, we who speak words that men will not be pleased to hear. Our very demeanor and appearance will be openly different from the increasingly "groovy" life style; we will clash with the sanctioned norms of this world, which, in the sight of God, are an abomination of decadence and sin. Just our appearance, our presence bringing with us something of the holiness of our Lord, will move men to irritation, anger, and worse.

Pits and Peaks: The Pattern and Rhythm of God

God allowed Joseph, the tender dreamer who was beloved

of the father more than all the sons, wearing the many-colored robe, to be tossed by his brothers into a pit. This incident is not meaningless happenstance, but seems to me to be the definitive pattern and working of God. It may well be that there are some of you, reading these words, who are finding yourselves this day in pits. They seem to be pits of circumstance, but they may be every bit as dark, lonely, and oppressive as the literal place in which Joseph found himself. These are places where every temptation is to be downcast, separated, isolated, pained, and perplexed. However, as we begin to consider the character and scope of our God, we can only be filled with the pure hope and certainty of His glory.

Joseph's brothers, after throwing him into a pit, brought him up again only to sell him for twenty pieces of silver to a passing band of Ishmeelites (Genesis 37:28). In the first verse of the thirty-ninth chapter of Genesis, we read,

> And *Joseph was brought down* to Egypt; and Potiphar, an officer of Pharaoh, captain of the guard, an Egyptian, bought him of the hands of the Ishmeelites, which had brought him down thither.
>
> (our italics)

It seems to me that there is an inevitable bringing-down before we are brought up. There is always a period of obscurity before God brings forth out of that darkness and isolation His Josephs for the age.

Where was God during Joseph's exile? "And the Lord was with Joseph . . ." (Genesis 39:2a). What an encouragement to know, in the depths of our dealings, when it seems to us that we are utterly isolated, forlorn, and cast down, that "the Lord was with Joseph. . . ." I wonder if he had the *sensation* of the Lord being with him, or, did he know that the Lord was with him solely because of his trust in His promises, and because of God's very nature and character? Many of us are beating our chests and crying "Oy vey" (or whatever the non-Jewish equivalent is), fearing that God is not with us, simply because we are carnal people, who have to *feel* to be convinced that something is true. Our Lord clearly tells us, ". . . lo, I am with you alway, even unto the end of the world," and, ". . . I will never leave thee, nor forsake thee" (Matthew 28:20b and Hebrews 13:5b, respectively).

> And the Lord was with Joseph, and he was a prosperous man; and he was in the house of his master the Egyptian.
> And his master saw that the Lord was with him, and that the Lord made all that he did to prosper in his hand.
> And Joseph found grace in his sight, and he served him: and he made him overseer over his house, and all that he had he put into his hand.
>
> Genesis 39:2-4

A pattern and a rhythm begin to be discernible; humiliation and being cast down, being brought up and finding favor and prosperity, and then—the dealings of God again. It's almost like breathing. God, who sees our hearts, knows how easy it is for us to be borne up on the stream of emotional exaltation, and how prone we are to attempt to steal portions of His glory. Perhaps it is for this reason that He has to bring us to a certain kind of rhythm of inflation and deflation, of moments of glory and moments of humiliation. We are tempered continually at His hand lest our fleshly hearts rise up.

At the End of the Ages

> And it came to pass from the time that he had made him overseer in his house, and over all that he had, that the Lord blessed the Egyptian's house for Joseph's sake; and the blessing of the Lord was upon all that he had in the house, and in the field.
>
> And he left all that he had in Joseph's hand; and he knew not ought he had, save the bread which he did eat. And Joseph was a goodly person, and well favoured.
>
> And it came to pass after these things, that his master's wife cast her eyes upon Joseph; and she said, Lie with me.
>
> Genesis 39:5-7

Joseph, favored above the other sons by his father Jacob, after being cast down into the pit and then raised up to prosperity in the house of Potiphar, was now brought face-to-face with an excruciating temptation. This is not just an historical episode, a page out of the life of a Jewish man of God, but a pattern to which we are going to be called increasingly at the end of the ages.

It was not long ago in a midwestern city, preceding a gospel conference, that I took a week out with another brother and went to a remote farm just to seek the face of the Lord in fasting and in prayer, in the hope that I might receive a new word for God's people. We prayed, we fasted, and we cried out to God and the heavens were as brass—not a word of answer. The week went by; still, we had not heard a word from the Lord. Finally, the convention began and I was downcast and wondering what I could possibly speak

7

about. Suddenly, while sitting at the first meeting, listening to another brother, the heavens opened and something came crashing down upon my heart. One statement: "End-Time Message." Something clicked in my soul. God did not give me a single new message, but everything I had been speaking all through the years had now been underlined, the i's dotted and the t's crossed: all had been vitalized with a new punctuation and urgency.

Joseph is an end-time message. Elijah is an end-time message. Job is an end-time message. There is not a thing now that I see in the Scriptures that does not pertain to the end times. To evade the perception that we are at the end of the ages can only lead to a grotesque distortion of one's vision, and to the missing of the most profound exclamations of God which would have prepared one for such an hour.

Although I am not a theologian, and probably could not make a formal defense of my position, I think it fair to tell you that I do not subscribe to the happy and convenient theology which says that God's people are going to be raptured and lifted up when a time of tribulation and trial comes. My experience contradicts it. The whole message of discipleship, preparation, and coming into the manhood, fulness, and maturity of Christ Jesus seems to me to be a preparation for such an hour. *Preparation*: this is the key. If it pleases God that such preparation need not be used, well, praise the Lord, let me just be lifted up in a more lean and muscular spiritual condition; better than going into the Kingdom with my spiritual gut hanging over my belt, burping and belching all the way.

Architects of the Modern World

Maybe it's because I'm on the front lines, in ministry with my own Jewish people, that I have such a strong presentiment of what the end times are going to mean to the

8

Body of Christ. The connection may seem vague. It is this: the Jewish people, God bless them, are eminently caught up in the spirit of this world. I'm not saying anything that's anti-Semitic; I'm just stating the blunt truth. They are the architects of the modern world. The whole world, not only the Western Hemisphere, is living, essentially, a Jewish life style. The great thinkers, pioneers, and shapers of it have been such men as Karl Marx, Sigmund Freud, and Albert Einstein, all Jews, and, strangely, all German. As we Jewish people know, there are few people more haughty than German Jews. Rightfully so, because they are endowed with fantastic brilliance, competence, and capability. We are living their life style. We subscribe to their theology, their psychology, and their method of child rearing. We even use their vocabulary. Speaking about complexes and inhibitions, we put aside the Ten Commandments and God's strict admonitions against infidelity, adultery, and fornication, and allow ourselves to be induced, day by day, into a groovier accommodation with sexual innovation and experimentation all because Freud or his latter-day disciples told us to "free" ourselves. The world has been shaken by a Karl Marx. We could not even recognize the twentieth century if his influence were omitted.

What shall we say of Albert Einstein? Sweet man that he was, he gave us the atom bomb, the very threat of which hovers over our entire civilization. There is something else that Einstein contributed which is even more explosive, fearful, and devastating, which is, physically speaking, not a bomb. Morally speaking, it is a bomb of great magnitude. It was born in the theory of relativity, and it is called *relativism*.

I myself was a leading exponent of it until God opened my eyes. I looked with great contempt upon the Bible. The idea of any single book holding up a standard for conduct and life is foolish and contemptible in the eyes of modern men. We relativists believed that truth was to be found in many sources and that one's entire lifetime was to be, necessarily, a quest for it.

The argument goes something like this: "Truth is not to be obtained, and you never come to the knowledge of it, but the nobility of striving is what counts. There is no foundation upon which any truth may be established, and no fixed point. *Everything is relative*. Who's to say whether something is right or wrong? After all, head hunting in the jungles of New Guinea is justifiable because it's relative to that culture; and who is to say that whatever you might do in the back seat of a car is wrong, by the same measure? I mean, after all, if it's *love*, who can say no?" The Bible and the counsel of God are rejected, and we go happily fornicating to our doom in the sweet rationalization that it's "love," when God said, "Thou shalt not."

In our lifetime, we are going to see an utter collapse of this elaborate civilization, which is already swaying and tottering. Its foundations have been severely undermined, and great cracks in its walls have become clearly visible. We are in the end times, and that civilization resting on the contributions of Jewish genius and rejecting the words and way of the Greater Jew shall pay a severe price. God is, as the darkness collects and the thick gloom comes, preparing a people to be a light and an instrument of salvation at the end of the ages: a Joseph people.

Revelation in Crisis

When we read the story of Joseph for the first time, we are held in great suspense as he stands before Potiphar's wife and her seductive invitation, "Lie with me." We know that, in this moment of critical trial and temptation, Joseph's character is, for better or for worse, about to be clearly displayed. It is always at moments like this that we see men and things most clearly.

The end times will be increasingly a period of unspeakable crisis. Paraphrasing the political science axiom, "Power corrupts and absolute power corrupts absolutely," I would say, "Crisis reveals and absolute crisis reveals absolutely." We are in an hour of revelation, of light; things which have all along been concealed, cloaked, and gilded over are now being revealed in all their stark proportions.

Take patsy religion, for example, and all our unctuous claptrap about "the three great faiths." There is not a modicum of faith to be found in any of them; they are religious establishments for the most part, religions of cultural convenience. We have spent our time exchanging pulpits on Mother's Day and Thanksgiving, congratulating ourselves for our benign attitude of tolerance one toward another, while, all this time, there is a God Who is *holy* calling us to *a Way*. In this age of revelation, as the turmoil, consternation, and dismay of the world break forth, all of these foolish things are going to slip away.

The collisions between light and darkness, between the Kingdom of God and the kingdom of this present world, are going to be nakedly revealed. There is not going to be any neutral ground to stand on, but only *two positions*: those who are in God, walking in His Way and reflecting His holiness, and those who have taken the lesser path. We will not be able to conceal things with labels in that day. We shall be *conspicuous* as the children of God, an accusation for the age. The "Jesus movement" is not going to be as groovy as it has been until this hour. Believing is not going to be a matter of dropping a dollar in the collection plate or attending a function; it is going to be a commitment unto death. Those who shall walk in the way of God shall find themselves increasingly brought down into "Egypt," into places of trial,

11

testing, and isolation. It is in these places that God fashions souls and enables them to know Him in the fellowship of His sufferings; and God shall bring each of these chosen and yielded vessels up in due season to be used as an instrument of His salvation.

But He Refused

"It came to pass after these things, that his master's wife cast her eyes upon Joseph; and she said, Lie with me" (Genesis 39:7). Have you been hearing that seductive call in these days? It's getting louder and louder. "Lie with me" is the summation of the whole enticing spirit of the age. Wherever you are susceptible, there will you hear it. Wherever you are moved in fleshly self-consideration, you are going to hear the most wily, seductive, and luxuriant voice, saying, again and again, "Come lie with me. Oh, you've got it coming. You deserve it. You're a red-blooded Jewish man, Joseph, who has never yet had an opportunity since your brothers cast you into the pit to experience and to express what every man should have *as a right*."

I can imagine how some of Joseph's brothers might have thought: "If I yield to this woman, this will prove to be an advantage later for my brethren. I'll be well insinuated with her. I have the advantage of her husband's esteem for me, and now *she'll* be in my corner also. I couldn't have it made better. What an advantage for later. Then *I* will really be in a position to help my Jewish brethren when a time of want will come." I, she, him, them: where is God in these confused considerations? This mentality, attitude, and spirit has largely motivated the activities of so-called Christians up until this hour. Much of our church life, programs, and devices have been just that kind of rationalization and compromise. "I'll make myself acceptable. I'll take advantage of this situation. It's not so great a compromise,

12

the Lord understands, and it will redound *later* to the benefit of all."

Joseph's response to the call of the temptress is stated in three beautiful words, "But he refused" (Genesis 39:8a). What a simple and mighty antithesis to the spirit of our age that tells us that we've got it coming, we deserve it, we need a break, we've been deprived long enough. Psychiatric therapists often counsel their patients to go out and engage in intercourse indiscriminately and at the drop of a hat. Many are led to believe that the experience of sex is all that is needed to relieve them of their inhibitions and bring them into a flow of life that will save them from their stunted and knotted conditions. We are told that every kind of act is permissible: "Do, Have, Live, Luxuriate, Engage Your Senses." That whole Babylonish spirit is beginning to pervade the earth with a "groovy" kind of life style of which many of God's children are being tempted to partake. If they have not yet, in fact, partaken, then they are fighting battles in their minds and spirits, hearing continually the seductive call of Potiphar's wife, "Lie with me."

Do you want to know what it means to be truly, *spiritually* "Jewish?" It is not measured by pastrami or Israel bonds. It is measured by such an intimacy and union with God that, in the moments of severest temptation and crisis, a man who knows His holiness will, like Joseph, *refuse* to be the bedfellow of the spirit of this world. This is a generation that has not been taught to say, "No!"

> *But he refused*, and said unto his master's wife,
> Behold, my master wotteth not what is with me in
> the house, and he hath committed all that he hath
> to my hand;
> There is none greater in this house than I;
> neither hath he kept back any thing from me but

thee, because thou art his wife: *how then can I do this great wickedness, and sin against God?*

Genesis 39:8, 9
(our italics)

If there is any conspicuous absence within the community of believers, it is an absence of the awesome fear of God. We don't live in the continual conscious affirmation of being in His holy presence. Our mouths are too glib, our amens and hallelujahs are too easy, and we walk too shallowly and cavalierly, because we have not the sense of His pervading holiness. We think that if we are out of the sight of our brethren, in our own "privacy," that we can somehow loosen our tie and allow ourselves certain kinds of indulgences that we would not permit if we were to be seen by others, as if we are not actually being seen by Him. In His sight, we are transparent. Nothing is concealed. "How then can I do this great wickedness, and sin against God?"

Spiritual Baseball versus Real Maturity

Often my Jewish people say to me, "Hey, are you trying to convert me?" I say, "No, dear brother. God is only wanting to make a *mensch* out of you." The word *mensch* means, literally, a man, and, by implication, a full-orbed, *mature* human being. What is maturity? We might define it as a disciplined, unyielding response to temptation in the moment of severest trial. A mature person is one whose mind is girded up, whose life is disciplined, who will not buckle when moments of temptation come.

"Well," my people say, "I have the Ten Commandments. I don't need your Jesus."

"Really," I enquire, "How ya doing?"

"Well," they say, "pretty good," having grown up in the baseball mentality which says that if you come up to the plate ten times and get three hits you're a candidate for the Hall of Fame.

"I'm trying. Doing pretty good; I'm hittin' like three out of ten." My heart burns within me at that point, because I know the truth that they don't know:

> The soul that sinneth, it shall die.
>
> Ezekiel 18:20a

> For there is not a just man upon earth, that doeth good, and sinneth not.
>
> Ecclesiastes 7:20

> For the wages of sin is death; but the gift of God is eternal life through Jesus Christ our Lord.
>
> Romans 6:23

James says that if we fail in one point of the law, we have failed in *all* (James 2:10). Even if you are batting .999, missing only one point, it's the same as if you had never connected with the ball at all. Somewhere in the depths and recesses of your life there is a place of reservation, self-love, and withholding from God. It may well be that your yielding to the other ninety-nine per cent has been an accommodation to things with which you agree anyway.

As an example, let's look at marriage. What does it mean to be submitted to one's husband if he is a sweet, loveable, docile, pleasant, agreeable, spiritual kind of man in whom there is no contention? Submission only means something when there is a conflict of will; here is the true test. Many women are applauding themselves, convinced that they are submitted to their husbands with a quiet and meek spirit, but they have never really been tested because their wills have not been crossed. We men, who may now be laughing smugly, stand in exactly the same relationship with God. Oh yes, we have consented to so much, we've paid our tithes, and we are agreeable, pleasant, and cordial. The Lord has perhaps not yet made such demands upon us that reveal the *depths* of our own self-love.

At the end of the ages, the issues are going to be so severe that every man is going to be found out where he lives. If crisis reveals the nature of the world's enmity against God, when the cloak shall be pulled back, it shall also fully reveal the condition of each Christian in that same moment. Many of us, well fed, comfortable, enjoying beautiful cars, nicely furnished homes, and all the lovely things that attend the present fellowship of the saints, can sing "Amen" and "Hallelujah" with great ease. The season for these joys may not last much longer. We have one condition now, but what shall our condition be in the moment of extremity? What shall be revealed then, when the power fails, as it did in New York a few hot summers ago? Men and women found themselves caught in giant skyscrapers between floors when elevators stopped running, blind in inky blackness, choking in suffocating heat, crowded together with other bodies, scrambling in panic and fury in an attempt *to save themselves*.

How many of us who unctuously wear crosses around our necks, proudly display them in our homes and church architecture, and attach them on suction cups to our dashboards, will understand its true signficance at that moment of revelation in crisis? Have we never known that the cross is a place of separation and *death* to self? It is the place of the slaying of that niggardly squeamish and squealing self-love that is deeply at the heart of every human being.

The Lamb and the Pig

God, as part of His plan to prepare a people for the tasks of the end times, has given to myself and a group of believers a plot of land in the northern Minnesota wilderness. The Lord's disciples there, who are today being molded, will one day be sent out to Israel, Germany, and other hard places of ministry. Art Katz, this Brooklyn Jew who had never so much as picked up a shovel, did not know what stretching barbed wire meant, and never had to care for a single animal, has now been inducted into a new kind of experience. For example, we had a convocation in the summer of 1974, and we decided to slaughter a lamb and a pig, then skewer them on a spit and roast them, in order to feed the three hundred people who had gathered for that conference. What a fantastic experience for a guy who was accustomed to seeing nice cuts of meat conveniently wrapped in neat cellophane packages, just waiting to be picked up at the supermarket. This is our situation in a nutshell: we have been living a cellophane life, a life of convenience. God is now going to call us to ruthlessly honest kinds of experience as He shapes us to be the Josephs for our generation.

When the knife was put to the throat of that lamb, hanging from its heels from the limb of a tree, the blood began to flow profusely. A Jewish girl, a disciple, standing nearby, inadvertently, without even thinking, from the depths of her being, cried out, "Ooh, it's not fair!" The Lord pinned her to the wall in an instant. She discovered a new kind of intimacy with God that night, confronting ultimate realities which, previously, she had consistently avoided. If she thought that the slaughter of the lamb was unfair, what did she really believe, deep down in her heart, about the death of the greater Lamb? "It's not fair!" In one statement, she was contradicting and putting at arm's length the whole way of God that involves sacrifice, the shedding of blood, and death.

Without these components, there can be no life.

> For the life of the flesh is in the blood: and I have given it to you upon the altar to make an atonement for your souls: for it is the blood that maketh an atonement for the soul.
>
> Leviticus 17:11

God had *me* lined up for the next experience—the killing of the pig.

I didn't understand what a pig was until I had to feed those ugly, stinking animals. If I ever thought of the virtues of being kosher, I thought of them then. What a loathsome, squealing animal; you have never seen a more greedy kind of a thing. When you bring them food, they don't even let you get to the trough. They swamp you, and, if you should somehow slip on the manure and go down, you're a dead duck. When you finally arrive at the trough and pour that stuff in, they are already standing in it with all four feet, jumping, nipping each other, and knocking each other over. They're pigs! I thought to myself as I stood there, "This must be the most absolutely economical way in which God, in His genius, has packaged protein. In the pre-refrigeration age, He gave the minimum amount of brain, nerve, and sinew to this animal in order to package the maximum amount of protein."

Yet, as minimal as the apparatus of intelligence is in the pig, the principle of survival is unbelievably tenacious. It took four men to get that animal down, and each able-bodied man was hanging onto a leg as that stubborn thing jerked. It wasn't at all like a lamb; it was definitely *not* going to lay down its life. Somebody had his foot on its head and neck, and that fat thing was still squirming and jerking. At that point, one of the brothers looked at me, handed me the knife, and said, "Art, would you like to—?" There was a sudden

18

and intense repulsion in my soul that took me by surprise. This shrinking back sprang from a strange kind of identification with that animal, down on its face, squealing and writhing and fighting for its life. The perception was clear and frightening: I saw too much of Art Katz in that animal.

I passed the knife to a brother who was experienced at this sort of thing, and he knew exactly where to put it.

Later, when we had that animal taken apart, all the entrails removed, he took out the heart and showed it to me. The knife had gone right into it, slitting it deeply, and yet the animal did not die immediately. It squealed and made a ruckus and writhed and contorted until practically the last drop of blood was out of its body. I never saw anything *die* so hard as that stubborn, filthy pig, squealing to the end. I had an unsettling thought: "My goodness, that's us! Decorous, quiet, well-behaved Christians, sitting nicely in our pews, giving to missionary endeavor, attending Bible studies and all sorts of lovely church functions, *but* deep inside there's a squealing pig, writhing, full of life, stubborn; and God is standing with His foot on its neck, and it's still not willing to give up the ghost."

"Be Ye Separate"

Satan is loosed in his fury for an hour; this is only the beginning of an age of temptations more formidable than mankind has ever encountered. We can expect such vile and despicable onslaughts of evil that only one who is submitted to that place of complete separation at the cross of Christ Jesus shall be able to give answer as my brother Joseph gave it: "But he refused . . . how then can I do this great wickedness, and sin against God?"

God is bringing us back to the place of the beginning.

> Even as Abraham believed God, and it was
> accounted to him for righteousness.
> Know ye therefore that they which are of faith,
> the same are the children of Abraham.
>
> Galatians 3:6,7

This is the definitive "Judaism" of God. Four centuries
before God thundered from Sinai, "Thou shalt not commit
adultery," there was a simple Jew named Joseph who knew
God so well in the fellowship of His suffering that he did not
need to be told what the Law was. God is bringing us to this
place. He does not want us to play the game by the numbers,
or to live by articulated rules and regulations. This is a walk
with God *by the Spirit*. "How then can I do this great
wickedness, and sin against God?"

> And it came to pass, as she spake to Joseph day
> by day, that he hearkened not unto her, to lie by
> her, or *to be with her*.
>
> Genesis 39:10
> (our italics)

I remember a couple of young people who came to me after
a meeting one night, wanting me to pray for them. They
thought that one day they might be married, but that was a
very distant consideration, and now they were having all
kinds of problems. Every time they were alone, they
succumbed to sexual temptation.

"Art, pray for us that we will not succumb to the
temptation."

"How foolish for me to pray for you," I replied, "if after
this prayer you're going to go into your car, be alone, and
establish the conditions by which temptation will inevitably
snare you." How many of us pray out of one side of our

20

mouths, while consciously allowing these dangerous conditions to be established and perpetuated in our personal life? We are told not to make any provision for the lusts of the flesh (Romans 13:14). Joseph *refused* to hearken to Potiphar's wife, to lie by her, or even *to be with her*. This was a place of separation that was absolute and total.

Don't think that Joseph's refusal came easily. I don't imagine that his temptress was an uninteresting, homely woman. I'm certain that here was a sumptuous temptation, the epitome of Egyptian sensuality. To turn away from her must have entailed such a wrenching pain for Joseph that we can hardly understand it if we have never considered resistance.

This walk is a call to separation, and separation is always an experience in suffering. If you have not the vaguest idea of what I mean, try fasting for a couple of days. Just deny the flesh its accustomed three squares a day with a little *nosh* (snack) in between, and you will hear a screech and a holler coming up from the subterranean depths of your life that you will not believe. You say that you have never heard that noise before. It never bothered you when you went to church or Bible study. It let you be a nice Christian, even "charismatic;" but the moment you begin denying the flesh and asserting the primacy, supremacy, and dominion of the Spirit, you will know that there is a fearful war going on.

Wherefore come out from among them, and *be ye separate*, saith the Lord, and touch not the unclean thing; and I will receive you,

And will be a Father unto you, and ye shall be my sons and daughters, saith the Lord Almighty.

2 Corinthians 6:17,18
(our italics)

21

The Fatherhood of God is not just a credo or a pious-sounding doctrine. We cannot know it by merely living a well-meaning, moderate, religious Christian life, in which mindless, habitual rituals usurp the place of true worship. If you have never known Him intimately as your Father, you may wonder why profuse streams of tears sometimes roll down the faces of believers as they worship God. There is no facile human method that can bring us to this knowledge, which comes only by the *presence* of the Holy One of Israel. It is only His presence, His reality, that can break your heart and bring you, in tears, on your face before Him. I relish every such time that God has brought me so low. We desperately need to know Him in this way, walking with Him, following Him, having come out from the darkness of this world and become *separate*.

The Reproach

And it came to pass about this time, that Joseph went into the house to do his business; and there was none of the men of the house there within.

And she caught him by his garment, saying, Lie with me: and he left his garment in her hand, and fled, and got him out.

And it came to pass, when she saw that he had left his garment in her hand, and was fled forth,

That she called unto the men of her house, and spake unto them, saying, See, he hath brought in an Hebrew unto us to mock us; he came in unto me to lie with me, and I cried with a loud voice:

And it came to pass, when he heard that I lifted up my voice and cried, that he left his garment with me, and fled, and got him out.

Genesis 39:11-15

Commitment to God meant nakedness, shame, reproach, and false accusation for Joseph; we are called to exactly the same pattern. Who more than our Lord Himself exemplified the truth of this phenomenon? We as His people must never be unmindful of Jesus' statements concerning the response of the world to our commitment to God.

> The disciple is not above his master, nor the servant above his lord.
> It is enough for the disciple that he be as his master, and the servant as his lord. If they have called the master of the house Beelzebub, how much more shall they call them of his household?
> Matthew 10:24,25

In 1973, a certain evangelistic program came out which stirred up all sorts of talk of "bringing Christ to the continent." It was a well-meaning intention, but, by the time it was all over, the actual fact turned out to be a pitiful little bleep—no more than a few bumper stickers. The Jewish community, however, rose up in intense indignation, as if there was some momentous aggressive campaign to convert every Jew. Rabbis and community officials fired fierce statements at Christians, many of whom drew back, cowering under the heat of the words and voices: "Say, what are you Christians trying to do? Haven't we Jews suffered enough in World War II? Weren't we exterminated by the millions? Aren't we struggling to preserve our Jewish identity in Russia? Are you, too, trying to make *Christians* out of us, and steal from us our Jewish identity?" I can still feel the blast of the ferocious response. Against these loud voices there was one still small voice that speaks eternally and says:

23

. . . Go ye into all the world, and preach the gospel
to every creature.

Mark 16:15

. . . Repentance and remission of sins should be
preached in his name among all nations, beginning
at Jerusalem.

Luke 24:47

. . . The gospel of Christ . . . is the power of God
unto salvation to every one that believeth; to the
Jew first, and also to the Greek.

Romans 1:16

The basic opposition which mankind is presented with will
increase in clarity as we press more deeply into the end
times: one still small voice, a sweet whisper out of the heart
of God, to those who have ears to hear, against which will
rage clamant, strident voices in great volume, saying, in
effect, "Come, lie with me."

As those believers in whom the Spirit of God dwells seek
to persuade my kinsmen to believe, they will be met by a
loud cry: "Why don't you leave them alone? Anti-Semite!
You call that Christian love?" There can be no greater irony,
no more bitter reproach and no falser accusation than this.
The child of the Lord, who loves the Jewish people, will, in
his faithfulness in serving God and them, receive the
reproach "anti-Semite" from people who don't have an iota of
concern for the actual condition of the Jews.

J had an experience on an airplane recently which
illustrates the kind of situation that we, as believers, can
expect. The plane was about to take off from Chicago, when
one last passenger came in, a young black woman, and sat

24

between me and a blonde lady in the third seat. Just as she sat down, something in my spirit went "Boing!" There is no compulsive urgency in me to witness to every person. I wait for the prodding of the Spirit, and when He speaks you can *know* that something is being worked for eternity.

As I sat in that airplane seat, however, God's Spirit moved within me, and I was engaging that women in conversation before the plane was hardly off the runway. I had a passionate interest in her life that was not born of me.

"What do you do?" I asked.

"I'm a student, a graduate student in psychology."

I found myself relating to her in an almost teasing manner thinking, "Katz, why are you speaking in this way?" I asked her, "What hope do you actually think that psychology holds for mankind, in its wretched and torn condition?" Her answers were weak and unassertive and soon we came to a place in the conversation where I said, "Have you considered the Bible as a standard for life and conduct?"

"Oh no," she said, "that's the white man's book. That's Uncle Tom religion, cop-out stuff!"

Somehow, in my spirit, I knew that, once upon a time, when she was a little girl, she had heard the Word and had known the Way of God, but had, with the passing years, been caught up in the spirit of the world in the form of that seductive black militant jive. She said to me at one point, "Me first, my people next, and the world last!" I thought to myself, "If the door should fly open, and Katz should be sucked out to oblivion and destruction, this girl would not so much as bat an eyelash." She was coming rapidly to the place of not having any natural affection; she was full of slogans and fierce, radical cries, and dehumanized already by the system. I'm not referring to capitalism, but to that system ruled over by Satan that beguiles and seduces the minds and spirits of men and women.

She was getting exasperated, and tried to shut me up, but I would not be shut up. I knew it was not Katz speaking. I had never spoken like that before; it was not according to the rulebook on how to witness to black people. Finally, in complete exasperation, she turned on me; this good looking woman said in a loud and painfully public voice, "If you don't stop, I'm going to call the stewardess and have your seat changed!" Her words broke very suddenly upon my soul, and I began to blush from the roots of my being right up to my hairline. I was beet red because, all of a sudden, it occurred to me that if, before a hundred or more passengers, a stewardess should come and change my seat, I was going to be made to look like I had made a pass at her—*Reverend* Katz.

It was now time for the blonde who was on the other side of my neighbor to lean over and look at me through thickly mascaraed eyes. Her lipstick was liberally smeared above her lip line, and a cigarette was hanging loosely from the corner of her mouth. "Yeah," she bellowed, "why don'tcha leave her alone?"

I thought, "Thank you, Lord. The picture is complete."

The very soul that you are seeking to save will be the one that will rise up in anger and perplexity against you. The people who are completely indifferent to the salvation of that soul, the nominal churchgoers, steeped in this world and its ways, who don't give one rap for my Jewish people or for the conditions of a lost mankind, will lean over and say, "Yeah, why don't you leave them alone?" They will boast of having done a good deed, and might even kill us and claim that this is, after all, a part of doing God's service.

We are looking at a pattern for the end of the ages. Every appearance will be deceiving to the natural mind. We are going to be looking, more and more, like obstacles to progress. Mankind, in agonizing desperation, will be looking for clever solutions for the crises and the dilemmas of the age, and in the way will stand this peculiar people insisting upon the narrow gospel of Jesus Christ. Internationally, the spiritual situation is essentially uniform: we can expect to be every bit as much of an impediment to *this* society as our brothers and sisters on the other side of the Iron Curtain are to that one. There are believers over there who are, even now, having their tongues yanked out of their mouths and their bodies pulverized and crushed because they will not bow to a system ruled by men who would have them deny the Lord who saved them. The Soviet authorities are threatened by the very existence of these peaceful people who submit to a higher Authority, Whose wisdom is foolishness to this world.

And she laid up his garment by her, until his lord came home.

And she spake unto him according to these words, saying, The Hebrew servant, which thou hast brought unto us, came in unto me to mock me:

And it came to pass, as I lifted up my voice and cried, that he left his garment with me, and fled out.

And it came to pass, when his master heard the words of his wife, which she spake unto him, saying, After this manner did thy servant to me; that his wrath was kindled.

And Joseph's master took him, and put him into the prison, a place where the king's prisoners were bound: and he was there in the prison.

Genesis 39:16-20

Joseph's garment in the hand of Potiphar's wife, a consequence of his innocence, his fleeing from temptation, became the very article of accusation and indictment used to cast him into the "pit" yet again. True to the pattern we have been observing, the concluding verses of this thirty-ninth chapter reveal the perpetual faithfulness of God and His inevitable raising up of His people, even within the physical context of prison walls:

> But the Lord was with Joseph, and shewed him mercy, and gave him favour in the sight of the keeper of the prison.
> And the keeper of the prison committed to Joseph's hand all the prisoners that were in the prison; and whatsoever they did there, he was the doer of it.
> The keeper of the prison looked not to any thing that was under his hand; because the Lord was with him, and that which he did, the Lord made it to prosper.
>
> Genesis 39:21-23

The Perplexity

We read in the fortieth chapter that the Pharoah's butler and baker, who were imprisoned in the same ward as Joseph and were in his charge, both had dreams during the same night. They were sad because they could not interpret their dreams and presented their problem forlornly to Joseph. His response was characteristic of the man who is confident of the presence and power of God:

> And they said unto him, We have dreamed a dream, and there is no interpreter of it. And Joseph said unto them, Do not interpretations belong to God? tell me them, I pray you.
>
> Genesis 40:8

28

Two years later, the Pharaoh had two dreams which utterly puzzled him. This was only the beginning of a greater perplexity, for this ruler called for every wise man in the entire country in a massive attempt to solve these mysteries.

> And it came to pass in the morning that his spirit was troubled; and he sent and called for all the magicians of Egypt, and all the wise men thereof: and Pharaoh told them his dream; but there was none that could interpret them unto Pharaoh.
>
> Genesis 41:8

We, in *this* age, are coming increasingly to such an hour of perplexity. Our expertise, our great knowledge, our councils of economic advisors, our IBM computers, our memory banks, and all the things upon which modern civilization has based its trust and its ultimate faith are going to prove to be completely useless. There won't be one wise man in "Egypt" who shall be able to give answer.

In the moment of confusion, the butler, who had been released from the prison two years earlier, remembered how God had given true interpretation of dreams through His servant Joseph. He quickly informed the Pharaoh of the prophetic utterances of the jailed Hebrew and of their perfect fulfillment. Once again, it was time for our man of God to be extricated from the pit.

> Then Pharaoh sent and called Joseph, and they brought him hastily out of the dungeon: and he shaved himself, and changed his raiment, and came in unto Pharaoh.
>
> Genesis 41:14

It will be the same in our time. In the moment of greatest perplexity, God is going to pluck out of obscurity, out of the prison in which He has been tempering the souls of His saints, a lowly "Hebrew" to give answer.

As he stood before Pharaoh, Joseph's integrity was unshaken. This man who belonged to God was swift to reject any belief that divine answers might originate within his own finite and fallible mind. Refusing the ultimate spiritual temptation, he pointed to the one true source:

> And Pharaoh said unto Joseph, I have dreamed a dream, and there is none that can interpret it: and I have heard say of thee, that thou canst understand a dream to interpret it.
> And Joseph answered Pharaoh, saying, It is not in me: God shall give Pharaoh an answer of peace.
> Genesis 41:15,16

God is preparing a people to stand like Joseph in the hour of perplexity, when everything is hanging on the line and the stakes are enormous. If we Josephs shall fail to refuse the spirit of this age and to be a people who know God by His Spirit, we will not, in that hour, be an instrument by which He can reveal His mysteries, and give answer to a desperate and needy world. God has called us to the way of revelation by His Spirit. "The answer is not in me," Joseph said. "God shall give you answer. Do not interpretations belong to God?" The Holy Spirit is not given to titillate us, to adorn our denominations, or to spice up our meetings. Paul writes:

> But we speak the wisdom of God in a mystery, even the hidden wisdom, which God ordained before the world unto our glory:

Which none of the princes of this world knew: for had they known it, they would not have crucified the Lord of glory.

But as it is written, Eye hath not seen, nor ear heard, neither have entered into the heart of man, the things which God hath prepared for them that love him.

But God hath revealed them unto us by his Spirit. . . .

1 Corinthians 2:7-10a

The Holy Spirit is not a plaything for religionists; He is the instrumentality through Whom those visions born in the heart of God are revealed to men. His presence and ministry are crucial, for "Where there is no vision, the people perish" (Proverbs 29:18a).

I would still be grasping for answers in darkness today, or might have already perished, had it not been for the mercy of God and the revelation by His Spirit. Great hotshot Art Katz was one of the "princes of this world:" Marxist, communist, atheist, pragmatist, existentialist, conversant in philosophy, able to speak on any subject. All you had to do was touch him and he would regale you with information, opinions, and every kind of notion of how to change the world. *But he could not change his own life.* As a man who had lived all his life in the power of intellect, and had worshiped at its Jewish shrine, I now tell you that intellect, human endowment, and human cleverness have not a cotton-picking thing to do with the revelation of God's mysteries. "But God hath revealed them unto us by his Spirit." God does not will that we abandon the intellect, but only that we sweep it off our altars and use it in the service of our Creator.

I began learning this lesson over a decade ago, in the

31

depths of my own crisis, aboard the deck of a Greek ship. A little book came into my hands that I would have scorned to read ever before; I thought of it as a "gentile" book. It was called the New Testament. In the first reading of that book, things of unspeakable profundity began to break upon my heart. What shattering exclamations came at me from the mouth of Jesus. Jesus. I was not even able to pronounce His name, so much was He a bone in my throat, yet I knew that no Jew ever spoke as this Jew spoke. There had never before been such an immense response in my soul as there was then to the statements that issued from Him, the magnitude of His being, the impeccable quality of His life and character, and, to my astonishment, the Jewishness of all of the men whom I had thought to be Gentiles, Jewish kinfolk like John and Peter. In my ignorance, I had previously thought that Jesus Himself was not a Jew, but I was reading of the greatest One who ever walked in a body of Jewish flesh and blood.

When I came to the line where Jesus says that He came not to destroy the law but to fulfill it (Matthew 5:17), I thought "How does He dare speak this way? What kind of chutzpah and arrogance is this? Who does He think He is? He speaks more than any rabbi or prophet would dare to speak. Forgiving men their sins! Letting men fall to His feet to worship Him! Who is this man?" The Spirit had begun to break ground in my soul.

Then that woman was taken in the act of adultery in the eighth chapter of John. My heart was pounding because I saw myself as one with her, caught in the sinful act, and I knew that I deserved what she deserved: the judgment of God—stoning, death. My heart was crying out for something I could not even identify. I did not know what to ask for or whom to ask for it. I was such an atheist and a cynic that I did not know what the word "mercy" meant. The sinner stood near my newly found hero in the midst of the accusing scribes and Pharisees, and I thought: "What is Jesus going to say now? He said that He came to fulfill the law and the law clearly prescribes 'death by stoning' for this offense." I closed the book and was afraid to read on, trying to think of some clever thing and bail Him out. My intellect ran up one side of the dilemma and down the other, thinking of every kind of answer, but it was all hopeless; there was no human answer at all to His predicament. I re-opened that book with trembling hands as I waited for the answer of my new Jewish hero, who was greater than a Karl Marx, a Sigmund Freud, or an Albert Einstein—heroes who had disappointed me, gods who had failed. The Scriptures described Jesus, He who had not a place to lay His head, bent over and poking His finger in the dirt. I pictured the face of the One who had never sinned contrasted with the faces of His accusers: self-righteous religious types, spittle running from the corners of their mouths, just waiting for an opportunity to do in this nuisance whose very presence was a living accusation against them. He looked up, with the woman shaking with fear at His feet, and said, "He that is without sin among you, let him first cast a stone at her" (John 8:7b). When that line floated up off the page and passed through my eyes into my brain, my body began trembling violently. It did not stop in my head, where I *thought* my life was, but moved down to where the true seat of life is, in the *heart*. I was cleaved in two by the power of God; the word that had issued out of the mouth of Jesus had divided my soul and spirit asunder. No merely human mind could have produced that divine wisdom. At that moment I knew with complete certitude, atheist that I was a moment before, that this was the Word of God. "There is, therefore, a God in heaven, and Jesus, therefore, must be Who He claims to be." I had received a revelation of the mystery of God.

33

"What do you mean?" my Jewish people say. "Father, Son and Holy Spirit—explain it!" I am incapable of supplying a good explanation. Paul himself wrote repeatedly of the *mystery* of the Godhead. It is to these mysteries that we are called.

> Let a man so account of us, as of the ministers of
> Christ, and stewards of the mysteries of God.
> 1 Corinthians 4:1

May God stop our mouths if we become too unctuous, too "spiritual," too eager to quote our favorite theologian. May God temper our souls and remind us of the great mysteries of the Lord that can only be revealed by His Spirit.

> . . . for the Spirit searcheth all things, yea, the
> deep things of God.
> For what man knoweth the things of a man,
> save the spirit of man which is in him? even so the
> things of God knoweth no man, but the Spirit of
> God.
> Now we have received, not the spirit of the
> world, but the spirit which is of God; that we might
> know the things that are freely given to us of God.
> 1 Corinthians 2:10b-12

"The answer is not in me," Joseph told the perplexed ruler. "God shall give you answer." And God gave answer, that men would not perish.

The One Crucial Question
Through Joseph, God revealed the meaning of Pharaoh's dreams: all the land of Egypt was about to experience seven

34

years of plenty followed immediately by seven years of famine. In this prophetic utterance, it was made clear that Egypt could avoid perishing by following specific guidelines laid down by God. The primary directive, that upon which all the rest hinged, was:

> Now therefore let Pharaoh look out a man discreet and wise, and set him over the land of Egypt.
>
> Genesis 41:33

After having witnessed the failure of all the wise men and magicians of Egypt and the success of a lowly Jewish man of God, Pharaoh understood the basic prerequisite for true discretion and wisdom:

> And Pharaoh said unto his servants, Can we find such a one as this is, *a man in whom the Spirit of God is?*
>
> Genesis 41:38
> (our italics)

It matters not at all whether you are a Presbyterian, Methodist, Baptist, Episcopalian, Pentecostal, or any such thing. I don't care whether you are a Jew or a Gentile. There is only one *crucial* question: Are you a man or woman in whom the Spirit of God is?

There is no such thing as spiritual neutrality. We receive our resources from either God or Satan. There is a fundamental decision to be made by every human being: "Which spirit shall I allow to come into and flood my life, to move and direct my being?" If we, as the people of God, shall choose Him freshly each day, even the Pharaohs of this world will say, as they gaze upon us, "Can we find such a one as this is . . . in whom the Spirit of God is?"

Such a one is far more than religious; this is one who has separated himself from the spirit of this world and offers himself *continually and fully* to the Spirit of God. We who have made this choice will be sneered at and called "fanatical." Accusations will be leveled against us. This choice will bring us to places that we never expected to find ourselves in, pits and dungeons; but, when it shall please God, at the end of the ages, He shall bring us forth as one man, a corporate Joseph, to give answer to a world that has none.

> And Pharaoh said unto Joseph, Forasmuch as God hath shewed thee all this, there is none so discreet and wise as thou art. . . .
>
> Genesis 41:39

Our university training, our human expertise, our so-called wisdom, can never make the crucial difference, can never provide the power to speak life to dying souls. It is only in the glory of God that we can find the life-giving, light-giving answer. Why?

> That no flesh should glory in his presence.
> But of him are ye in *Christ Jesus, who of God is made unto us wisdom, and righteousness, and sanctification, and redemption:*
> That, according as it is written, He that glorieth, let him glory in the Lord.
>
> 1 Corinthians 1:29-31
> (our italics)

It is in the places of greatest extremity that we discover that our own powers, knowledge, and abilities are not enough,

36

and that if we do not allow God to be made unto us divine wisdom and utterance, we shall surely perish. It is His divine power that " . . . hath given unto us all things that pertain unto life and godliness. . . " (2 Peter 1:3a).

Paul wrote, "For to me to live is Christ. . . " (Philippians 1:21a). He did not go about establishing churches on the basis of his intellectual endowments, but on the solid foundation of divine truth which enabled him to make the very radical statement:

> I am crucified with Christ: nevertheless I live; yet not I, but Christ liveth in me: and the life which I now live in the flesh I live by the faith of the Son of God, who loved me, and gave himself for me.
>
> Galatians 2:20

Too often these words have become for us merely a piece of theology, a pretty quotation from Scripture, or even a jolly-sounding little ditty which sounds somewhat like a television commercial. The apostle is giving us a vital message which must *sober* us before we can truly rejoice: "That selfish, squealing, cantankerous, demanding pig of self-life has really been brought to the cross, and has been cut away, once and for all. Its clamant demands on my life have been put away, crucified and buried with Christ, and it is no longer I that live, but Christ that lives in me." This is the statement of earnest believers at the end of the ages and there is no other.

If Joseph had lived for himself, he would have said yes to Potiphar's wife, but this man, in whom the Spirit of God dwelled, refused. In the dual act of refusal to the world's seductions and submission to the Lord, pigs are slain, angels rejoice, and God gains vessels through whom He can speak

His answers. In Genesis 41:45, we learn of the new name that Pharaoh gave Joseph—Zaphnath-paaneah, which has two meanings, both of which our ancient brother fulfilled: *the man to whom secrets are revealed* and *a revealer of secrets*. What God had revealed to His servant by His Spirit, His servant revealed to a people in need.

Unto a Perfect Man

> *. . . Touch not mine anointed, and do my prophets no harm.*
>
> *Moreover he called for a famine upon the land: he brake the whole staff of bread.*
>
> *He sent a man before them, even Joseph,* who was sold for a servant:
>
> Whose feet they hurt with fetters: he was laid in iron:
>
> Until the time that his word came: the word of the Lord tried him.
>
> The king sent and loosed him; even the ruler of the people, and let him go free.
>
> He made him lord of his house, and ruler of all his substance:
>
> To bind his princes at his pleasure; and teach his senators wisdom.
>
> Psalm 105:15-22
> (our italics)

There is famine coming upon the land. God is going to break the whole staff of bread. All of this glittering civilization and all of its accouterments and endowments, all of its lush affluence and prosperity will be shaken and *broken* by the hand of God. If you are suffering difficult and painful conditions in your life today, do not wonder if God has deserted His child. The Lord was with Joseph in the deepest pits and on the highest peaks. He promises to each of us no lesser faithfulness. It is God who sees your heart and your willingness to walk with Him, and is preparing you even now to be part of that man that He shall bring forth when the whole staff of bread is broken, and a perplexed world shall not have answers from its magicians and wise men.

"He sent a man before them, even Joseph." God is sending a man, a many-membered man, a corporate man. He is knocking down the things that have divided us; our denominational labels, our foolish theologies, our doctrines, our isolationism, our privacy, and our fears. He is tempering us together and making of us one people by dealing with us personally and privately, and dealing with us corporately.

> And Joseph was thirty years old when he stood before Pharaoh king of Egypt.
>
> Genesis 41:46a

Jesus, too, was thirty years old when He began His public ministry, the Lamb in the maturity of years. It is to Him we must look

> Till we all come in the unity of the faith, and of the knowledge of the Son of God, unto a perfect man, unto the measure of the stature of the fulness of Christ:
>
> That we henceforth be no more children, tossed to and fro, and carried about with every wind of doctrine, by the sleight of men, and cunning craftiness, whereby they lie in wait to deceive;
>
> But speaking the truth in love, may grow up into him in all things, which is the head, even Christ:

From whom the whole body fitly joined together and compacted by that which every joint supplieth, according to the effectual working in the measure of every part, maketh increase of the body unto the edifying of itself in love.

Ephesians 4:13-16

He is going to bring forth a man, in his maturity, unto a perfect man, in the fulness of the stature of Jesus Christ. Sober-minded, that man will be rich in his understanding of God *by the Spirit*, strongly walking in the fulness of that Spirit, and willing to submit to the dealings of His hand. All parts of that man will move gracefully together, united in His purpose, listening for His still, small voice. Having ended all commerce with the beckoning, taunting spirit of this world, the members of that man, by the merciful guidance of their Head, shall attain to that level of *maturity* through which God can speak and act. There is no way to obtain it without first, like Joseph, being brought down into "Egypt," and God shall not pull you there against your will.

If you will be satisfied with some lesser walk, the dollar in the collection plate for the endowment of pews, you can have it. If you want to pour some oil on the rocks, as Jacob did, and call *that* the House of God, you can have it. God, however, is looking for people who are dreamers and visionaries, who have eyes to see the world being increasingly steeped in darkness, whose hearts cry out for the Shechinah glory of God to break forth upon the earth, and who are willing to be the vessels of that Light at any price.

May we, as His people, never forget or take lightly the price our God paid in precious blood, that we might be saved from bondage, darkness, and death:

And that he died for all, that they which live

40

should not henceforth live unto themselves, but unto him which died for them, and rose again.

2 Corinthians 5:15

The world spirit will come to us more and more during these end times, and whisper, cry, sing, squeal, and shout, "Lie with me." The invitation may offer literal fornication, or a respectable-looking substitution of religious appearances for the vitality of a committed service to the living God. It will offer whatever might have the greatest potential to shift our eyes from His purpose to our desires. The result of saying yes is the same in every case: the forfeiture of our usefulness as an instrument for His revelation at the end of the ages.

That lowly Hebrew did not know that the entire world would be critically affected by his response to the seductive invitation of Potiphar's wife. Joseph's loving obedience to the Lord and his resistance to temptation resulted in God having a man through whom He could minister life to all nations in a time of great want.

And the seven years of dearth began to come, according as Joseph had said: and the dearth was in all lands; but in all the land of Egypt there was bread.

And when all the land of Egypt was famished, the people cried to Pharaoh for bread: and Pharaoh said unto all the Egyptians, Go unto Joseph; what he saith to you, do.

And the famine was over all the face of the earth: And Joseph opened all the storehouses, and sold unto the Egyptians; and the famine waxed sore in the land of Egypt.

And all countries came into Egypt to Joseph for

to buy corn; because that the famine was so sore in all lands.

Genesis 41:54-57

If Joseph was a man who had lived for himself, he would have embraced the devil's visible offer, and turned his back on his unseen Lord. Countless lives, history, hung in the balance at the moment of decision. God did not offer any deal to His man: He did *not* say, "If you refuse this woman, I will make you lord and ruler of Pharaoh's house and of all his possessions." All Joseph knew at the time was that to hearken to, lie by, or even *be* with his temptress would have constituted a great wickedness and a revolt against the very Spirit within him.

God is calling His people to simple obedience and a trusting walk with Him by the Spirit. We need not receive any immediate explanations or forecasts of consequences at the moment that He points the direction and, in His great faithfulness, says to us, "This is the way, walk ye in it" (Isaiah 30:21a).

That same spirit who spoke through Potiphar's wife to Joseph spoke also to our Lord Himself through Peter, and in effect, said, once again, "Lie with me."

From that time forth began Jesus to shew unto his disciples, how that he must go unto Jerusalem, and suffer many things of the elders and chief priests and scribes, and be killed, and be raised again the third day.

Then Peter took him, and began to rebuke him, saying, Be it far from thee, Lord: this shall not be unto thee.

But he turned, and said unto Peter, Get thee behind me, Satan: thou art an offence unto me: for thou savourest not the things that be of God, but those that be of men.

Matthew 16:21-23

At the cross, human flesh meets with the antithesis and utter defeat of every one of its selfish goals. The disciple was asking Jesus to consider the comfort and preservation of His earthen vessel. Peter's appeal may sound to many ears like the noblest of sentiments. If Jesus had said yes to it and avoided the cross, all of mankind, throughout all time, would have lost its only means of eternal salvation.

But He refused.

Chapter Two

As the Lord God of Israel Liveth, before Whom I Stand: Elijah and the End Times

The Statement

We hear nothing about God's great man Elijah before his abrupt introduction at the very beginning of the seventeenth chapter of 1 Kings. We see him there, in all the fulness and power of the Holy Spirit, standing before Ahab with complete fearlessness, speaking words of awesome intensity:

> And Elijah the Tishbite, who was of the inhabitants of Gilead, said unto Ahab, As the Lord God of Israel liveth, before whom I stand, there shall not be dew nor rain these years, but according to my word.
>
> 1 Kings 17:1

This verse is like the blowing of a trumpet. It is the presentation of an unheard-of man onto the stage of history in a perfect moment in the timing of God. I love God's discretion; it does not please Him to raise the curtain and let us see what it took to prepare and shape such a vessel as Elijah. There is only silence and obscurity.

We can safely assume that the spiritual mountain peak on which this prophet stood could have only been preceded by the "pit" of God's dealing. For men like Joseph and Elijah, submitted in their hearts to the will of God, each pit is a school of the Spirit, where, progressively and gradually, every confidence in the flesh is exposed and cut away. Before our Lord brings His disciples before the Pharaohs and Ahabs of this world, there must always be a period of crucial preparation in obscurity.

This pattern is true even of our Lord Himself. Except for a few incidents surrounding His birth and one youthful episode in the temple at Jerusalem, we know not a thing about the first thirty years of His life. Silence. Obscurity.

Maybe that's where our life is now, individually and corporately, as the Body of Christ. Unseen and in places unknown to others, the Lord is dealing with us and bringing us low—into pits.

"There shall not be dew nor rain these years, but according to my word." What manner of man is this who presumes to command the elements? This would be an act of unspeakable gall, chutzpah (arrogance) of embarrassing proportions, if Elijah was not so wholly hidden in God. In effect, it was not even he who was speaking, but the God Who possessed his life. In the yoke of loving obedience, God and His servant could work together in perfect unity, for ". . . he that is joined unto the Lord is one spirit" (1 Corinthians 6:17). It is to this place of intimate union with Him that the Lord is bringing those who are *willing* in the present hour, and the shaping of such vessels is not accomplished in one day.

Elijah was not afraid that he might be accused of infringing upon God or of attempting to steal His glory. He spoke boldly, for he knew that the two halves of his statement are perfectly related. There is no way that a man can command the elements without first affirming "As the Lord God of Israel liveth, before whom I stand."

To stand before the Living God means being closed in with Him while being separated from the world. Yet, this is only part of the implication, the easier part; the more fearful and demanding aspect entails separation not only from the world but sometimes even from your own brethren in the faith. Many of us have graduated from worrying about what the world says of us. We don't give a rap about that, and can well receive *their* reproach. Have we, however, come to a place of such maturity that we can live with the scorn of our brothers? That is not an easy place to come to, because we have perhaps just begun to really enjoy the prestige and acceptance of men, in this case, *Christian* men. The man who can stand before the King Ahabs of this world has got to be that one who stands before God continually. He must ultimately be indifferent to the opinions of both the world and those who call themselves by the Lord's name.

I am neither encouraging you to rebellion nor to looking askance upon the elders whom God has placed over you. In fact, I am deeply committed to the principle of submission to authority, and to all of the principles of relationship within the Body of Christ which are clearly delineated in the Scriptures. Yet, in the same breath, I must stress that there is required of every child of God an independence of the spirit and a tenacious cleaving and fidelity to the Lord, even when a situation might arise where it is seemingly impossible to give those closest to you an acceptable explanation.

The Way of Jeroboam

The magnitude of Elijah's act of speaking his strong words to Ahab can be appreciated all the more when we consider the character of that king. We read that:

> . . . Ahab the son of Omri *did evil in the sight of the Lord above all that were before him.*
>
> And it came to pass, as if it had been a light thing for him *to walk in the sins of Jeroboam* the son of Nebat, that he took to wife Jezebel the daughter of Ethbaal king of the Zidonians, and went and served Baal, and worshipped him.
>
> And he reared up an altar for Baal in the house of Baal, which he had built in Samaria.
>
> And Ahab made a grove; *and Ahab did more to provoke the Lord God of Israel to anger than all the kings of Israel that were before him.*
>
> 1 Kings 16:30-33
> (our italics)

48

The abundance of evil that existed in the reign of Jeroboam became a standard of darkness by which the apostasy of each succeeding ruler was measured. Nadab, Baasha, Elah, Zimri, Omri: each of these kings walked in that way, and with each one the extremity of Israel's departure from holiness was increased. Of all these black-hearted despots, Ahab was the worst. His wife Jezebel had singlehandedly seen to the execution of almost all of God's prophets. Elijah was the only one left. It is before *that* man that he stood, making, with resolute calm and boldness, that statement which is illustrative of his entire ministry.

The way of Jeroboam is not just an historical document, but is, most significantly for us, a vivid description of the future.

> Whereupon the king [Jeroboam] took counsel, and made two calves of gold, and said unto them, *It is too much for you to go up to Jerusalem*: behold thy gods, O Israel, which brought thee up out of the land of Egypt.
>
> 1 Kings 12:28
> (our italics)

If you have ever been to Israel, you are probably familiar with the very steep ascent to Jerusalem. Going up is a very *literal* going up. Three times each year, every male in Israel was required to go up for three essential feasts that required attendance at Jerusalem (see 1 Kings 9:25). Here, however, was a king who was going to make it easier by giving the Israelites a couple of golden calves, conveniently located, that they need not go up.

49

> And he made an house of high places, and made priests of the lowest of the people, which were not of the sons of Levi.
>
> 1 Kings 12:31

My guess is that Jeroboam may have established a few seminaries, passed men through their career courses, and given them pulpits. These men were not of the Levites; *they were not God's appointed messengers*. In short, their ministries were not born in heaven.

I had never wanted to call myself "minister." Getting me ordained was not a quick, easy work of God. I desired neither ordination nor organization; I just wanted to be God's man.

Early in my Christian life, I found myself in Kansas City, working with a pioneer evangelistic work in that area. Shortly after I had arrived in town, I attended a midweek morning service for local ministers. When those conducting the meeting called the ministers up to the platform, I did not budge, and was utterly determined to remain amongst the rest of the congregation. There was no way that I could presume, before God, men, or myself, to be in the same category as that group assembled in the front of the room. I had not even gone to seminary; I was just a Jewish layman from Brooklyn who had been drafted.

A few of the men who had already come to know me suddenly began beckoning from the platform, something to the effect of, "Come on, Katz. No copping out now. You come on up here with us." Uncomfortable and embarrassed, I went up, and they had me say a few words about my work there.

Just as I was about to sit down, a man came up from behind, another minister. He put his hand on my shoulder,

and said, "Brother, I have a word for you from the Lord."
God spoke to me with thundering love through the prophetic
utterance that followed: "Let him not think, whom I have
called to be My minister, that he is *not* My minister." The
Lord went on from there, and by the time He was finished
speaking, I was dissolved in a puddle of tears. From that day
forth, I have never again denied that I am a minister.

There are countless functionaries and religious
practitioners running rampant in this age. There is a world
dying because of the false equation of that self-ordained
group with the representatives of the Most High God. We
have not yet seen the end of the ways of Jeroboam.

There is a world church that is going to be formed that will
preach a religion of convenience. In it, you shall not have to
sweat to go up to Jerusalem; everything shall be easily
accessible, and nothing shall be required of you. Dropping a
dollar in the collection plate will suffice to ease the
whimperings of conscience. The men who shall minister in
its temples shall perhaps speak the conventional
terminology, but *they shall not know God*. Such men are not
"Levites," not God's priests. There is but one true
priesthood; it is comprised of all those who have been born
again of the Spirit, and who are wholly cleaving to the Living
God:

> But ye are a chosen generation, *a royal
> priesthood*, an holy nation, a peculiar people; that
> ye should shew forth the praises of him who hath
> called you out of darkness into his marvelous light:
> Which in time past were not a people, but are
> now the people of God: which had not obtained
> mercy, but now have obtained mercy.
> 1 Peter 2:9, 10
> (our italics)

The false priesthood of this world shall enmesh itself in a particular type of worship. It is nothing new:

> And Jeroboam ordained a feast in the eighth month, on the fifteenth day of the month, *like unto the feast that is in Judah*, and he offered upon the altar. So did he in Beth-el, sacrificing unto the calves that he had made: and he placed in Beth-el the priests of the high places which he had made.
>
> 1 Kings 12:32
> (our italics)

That feast was counterfeit; it appeared to be, but it was not, the real thing ordained of God in His time.

The configuration of false gods, false priests, and false worship is a perfect picture of the "church" which is going to be raised up in the end times. The foundation of that structure has already been laid.

The world at the end of the tenth century B.C. had never seen a fuller expression of the way of Jeroboam than in the reign of Ahab. In his marriage to Jezebel we witness the union of politics and religion. The Zidonians practiced a form of religion which had idolatry and orgiastic self-indulgence at the heart of it. It is before a configuration such as this that God is going to bring a people who will stand like Elijah, and speak the word of the Lord.

The Voice of the Master

> And the word of the Lord came unto him, saying,
>
> Get thee hence, and turn thee eastward, and hide thyself by the brook Cherith, that is before Jordan.
>
> And it shall be, that thou shalt drink of the brook; and I have commanded the ravens to feed thee there.
>
> 1 Kings 17:2-4

Had not Elijah been so joined to the Lord, he might have thought, upon receiving this word, "Uh oh, that's not God's voice. I'm wise to wiles of the enemy; I know what he's up to. That devil just wants to get me out into the wilderness and divert me from my appointed task. And ravens! Why, that's the last kind of instrumentality an all-wise God would use to feed His prophet. They're birds of prey, scavengers, garbage eaters. This is obviously just a satanic attempt to destroy me." But we read at the beginning of the next verse: "So he went and did according unto the word of the Lord" (verse 5a).

How did Elijah know that he was hearing the voice of the Lord? He knew in the only way that any of us can: he was familiar with the accents, the tone, the character of his God. That familiarity and knowledge is not born in a day, but is the result of repeated hearings and repeated acts of obedience.

I once spoke on the subject of God's still small voice at an open-air meeting on the campus of a California college. At the completion of the talk some radical students, wholly vexed by my presentation, came over to me. One of them snarled, "How do you know if you're hearing God's voice or

Satan's?" I thought, "The children of this world are wiser than the children of light. Would to God that God's children would ask such questions as this." I stroked my chin, trying to think of an answer. I did not have a little instant handbook, with alphabetically arranged sets of questions and answers, to quickly consult: "Let's see, V, voice." No. I am a completely hopeless character unless God be made unto me wisdom and knowledge.

Under my breath, behind my chin-stroking hand, I prayed, "Lord, give me wisdom. Speak to this boy. He's asking a crucial question." In that moment, my eye fell on a big shaggy mutt moving through the many knots of people who were still standing around. There was a noisy confusion in that place, a tumult of many heated voices. In the midst of all that, that dog was not just aimlessly wandering; it was moving on course, right on target. I said to my inquirer, "Say, fella, you see that mutt? It's not even a pedigree, but in this chaotic welter of voices, it has heard the voice of its master, and it's going." Elijah too heard his Master's voice *so he went and did according unto the word of the Lord.*

Are we, as His people, willing to take the chance of believing, acting, and then discovering that we have *missed* God's true direction? This might sound scary, but I'll tell you something wonderful about our God: He will always bail you out.

I was leaving a meeting one night, wholly tired and spent, and couldn't think straight. I was only thinking of getting to a bed. As I was just about to get out of that room, a woman clutched at my sleeve as I went by.

"Brother Katz?"

"Yes."

"Will you answer one question for me?"

"I'll try."

"On the way to the meeting tonight, as I was driving by

54

myself, there was a hitchhiker by the side of the road, and for the first moment, I had an impulse to pick him up. Then the thought came to me, 'How would it look for a Christian woman all by herself in a car, picking up a strange man?' And I didn't do it. What should I have done?"

She looked at me expectantly. I just gazed back at her with my tired eyes and said without even thinking (which is when I am at my best—or, more accurately, when His perfection meets with the least interference from me), "I believe that you should have stopped to pick him up. *If your life is surrendered to the Lord and if it's His to command*, you should obey that first impulse. I'll tell you what—even if it would have been a mistake, the Lord would have redeemed it."

He is the great Redeemer. God shall use even the errors of those who have acted out of real love for Him to teach them how to better discern His voice. How else shall we learn?

> And we know that all things work together for good to them that love God, to them who are the called according to his purpose.
>
> Romans 8:28

Getting to know the Lord's voice is inextricably linked to understanding His *way*. Why would God choose ravens to feed a prophet? How foolish and illogical. Yet God will choose those things which are foolish in the world's estimation to confound the worldly-wise (see 1 Corinthians 1:18-31).

I would have been suspicious if the voice which Elijah heard had said, "There shall be a Jewish caterer to sustain thee with three square meals a day, a nosh before bedtime, and the best gefilte fish this side of the Jordan." When I heard "ravens," I thought, "Ah, that's my God."

He is a God Who chose, when He penetrated time-space history in bodily form, to be born in a stable. Almost all of the Jews of that generation rejected their King. They knew neither the voice of God nor His distinctive way. There is nothing more necessary for the people of God of our generation than the appropriation of that knowledge which comes as a consequence of walking with the Author of grace day after day and year after year.

Kneeling at the Dried Brook

So he went and did according unto the word of the Lord: for he went and dwelt by the brook Cherith, that is before Jordan.

And the ravens brought him bread and flesh in the morning, and bread and flesh in the evening; and he drank of the brook.

And it came to pass after a while, that *the brook dried up*, because there had been no rain in the land.

1 Kings 17:5-7
(our italics)

What kind of God is this, anyway? He brings the prophet to a brook, a place of security, well-being, and provision, and then allows that brook to dry up! In the twelve years that I have walked with my Lord, He has repeatedly shown me that this is His characteristic way.

The first few years of my life with the Lord were marked by an unheard-of (in *my* life) security. I was a professional history teacher with tenure in a California high school—I couldn't be fired! For most of my existence, I had known almost nothing but urban struggle and insecurity. I rarely had a steady job in my life, and would flit from one short stint to another. Finally, this grown-up Depression baby had it made—career guaranteed, master's degree, annual wage increments, retirement benefits, medical insurance, ownership of our first house, and a nice little four-cylinder Chevy II—the whole bit. Nine years ago, while ensconced in all of that, God said, "Get thee out and follow Me."

I was to join a Christian organization and receive a hundred bucks a week with no fringe benefits and no guarantees—and Inger was pregnant with our third child. The prospect before me was totally foreign to my experience, and thinking about it would cause me to shudder with dread anticipation: I was being asked to stand on a soap box in the middle of New York City to preach the gospel of *Yeshua Hamasheach*. Talk about foolishness! How could I expect anything but abject failure! Yet, on the day that we departed from California en route to New York, I knew that I was being sustained by angels and could feel the breath of God on my neck.

We stayed with that group for four years until God separated us again and sent us to Europe. Although we were cut off from the security of official affiliation with the programs of that organization, they continued to send us a salary and even provided us with a car. I have not forgotten their general secretary turning to me and saying, "You know, we've never done anything like this before." God's ordained ways of provision for His people shall never be confined to the world's idea of "how it's done."

After a while, that stream dried up and we returned to the states from Europe and Israel with no organization, no salary, no visible security. *Nothing* but the promises of God.

In our first year back, we had our largest income ever, a seventeen-room house in New Jersey, two Volvos, every expense paid, and a television series called *The Ben Israel*

Program. In truth, we were neither richer nor more secure *then* than we were when God had stripped us of everything save His word.

I have been made to see that I never did receive my salary or security from a Board of Education or from an evangelical organization. They were instrumentalities that God used for a season.

> Every good gift and every perfect gift is from above, and cometh down from the Father of lights, with whom is no variableness, neither shadow of turning.
>
> James 1:17

My provision today does not come from God's people; it comes *through* them, from above. The Lord provides for His children through whatever agency pleases Him in any given moment. If a particular brook dries up, it makes no essential difference. God shall sustain you in yet another way.

The lesson is simple: don't look down to "brooks"—*look up to the Father of lights*. Looking down was the hang-up of the Chaldeans. Ur of the Chaldees, birthplace of Abram, was situated on the banks of the Euphrates River. The natives of that place were utterly dependent upon that body of water for their commerce and culture—indeed, for their life itself! God called Abram away from that visible source. He no longer looked down to that river. God's friend raised his eyes upward to the promise of a land of early and latter rains. Some time after his departure, the Euphrates diverted its course ten miles from that city, and Ur of the Chaldees perished. We have the same phenomenon historically along the Mississippi River in America; its flow shifted, and cities which had been flourishing centers of trade sounded their death rattles.

God is preparing us *now* for total dependence on Him, and is weaning us from every kind of thing in which we have found a false security. Every brook that we have worshiped and consider to be the *source* of our nourishment shall be, by our God's merciful hand, utterly dried up.

So He Arose and Went

And the word of the Lord came unto him [Elijah], saying,

Arise, get thee to Zarephath, which belongeth to Zidon, and dwell there: behold, I have commanded a widow woman there to sustain thee.

1 Kings 17:8, 9

How would the natural mind, still hankering after that Jewish caterer, respond to this command? "Oh, come on, Lord. Listen to reason. This is not even a Jewish woman you're sending me to. It was bad enough with that raven business, but Zidon is where Jezebel herself comes from. Those heathen know no limits to their wickedness, and right now they are suffering in the famine that I myself proclaimed. Now, really Lord, is that Zidonian woman going to sustain a Hebrew prophet? Never happen!"

The Scripture says of Elijah, "So he arose and went to Zarephath" (verse 10a). As many times as I read those words, great delight springs up in my soul. Sometimes, I say to people, half-jokingly, "If you have something to do with my burial and you want to put a nice inscription on my tombstone besides 'Arthur Katz, date of birth, date deceased,' one quotation will do beautifully: 'So he arose and went,' or, perhaps, 'So he went and did according unto the word of the Lord.' " My prayer is that such a statement may be, in the final analysis, a true description of my time on this earth.

So he arose and went, no ifs, no ands, no buts, no maybes, no arguing with God, no scratching his head and reviewing all the good, logical reasons why God's commandment could not possibly be fulfilled. Such a man, I repeat, is not fashioned in a day, and the shaping process is not necessarily pleasant. Every one of us has a craven heart, itching for a facile security, and reluctant to be separated from the egotistical hang-ups and fleshly cravings upon which we have built our lives.

Without spiritual heart surgery by the hand of God, there can be no standing before Ahab, and no life of sustained yieldingness to our Lord's bidding. Cutting away is never painless, but when God holds the scalpel the motive is clear, and the victory is sure:

> And the Lord thy God will circumcise thine heart, and the heart of thy seed, to love the Lord thy God with all thine heart, and with all thy soul, that thou mayest live.
>
> Deuteronomy 30:6

See, Thy Son Liveth

> So he arose and went to Zarephath. And when he came to the gate of the city, behold, the widow woman was there gathering of sticks: and he called to her, and said, Fetch me, I pray thee, a little water in a vessel, that I may drink.
>
> And as she was going to fetch it, he called to her, and said, Bring me, I pray thee, a morsel of bread in thine hand.
>
> And she said, As the Lord thy God liveth, I have not a cake, but an handful of meal in a barrel, and a

little oil in a cruse: and, behold, I am gathering two sticks, that I may go in and dress it for me and my son, that we may eat it, and die.

1 Kings 17:10-12

We see here a woman who is dying of much more than physical starvation. This is a picture of a person who is disconsolate, broken, disillusioned, and depressed. There is the suggestion of one who had lived "high on the hog," one who had enjoyed affluence, comfort, and luxury, and who had, all of a sudden, had the bottom pulled out from under her. That widow is a good representation of the world to which God shall send us in an Elijah-type ministry at the end of the ages.

After the crash of 1929, men and women committed suicide in record numbers. We can expect to see a repeat performance of this kind of response when economic catastrophe strikes again. Our generation has not been fitted to hold up under conditions of famine. Dispirited, it shall be ready to eat its last meal, roll over, and die.

And Elijah said unto her, Fear not, go and do as thou hast said: but make me thereof a little cake first, and bring it unto me, and after make for thee and for thy son.

For thus saith the Lord God of Israel, The barrel of meal shall not waste, neither shall the cruse of oil fail, until the day that the Lord sendeth rain upon the earth.

And she went and did according to the saying of Elijah: and she, and he, and her house, did eat many days.

And the barrel of meal wasted not, neither did

the cruse of oil fail, according to the word of the
Lord, which he spake by Elijah.

1 Kings 17:13-16

This miraculous provision, confirming the truth of the
prophetic word spoken by Elijah, was still not enough to
effect the salvation of the widow woman. She may have been
grateful to the prophet, and perhaps even to God, for the
physical sustenance, but, spiritually, there was no
regeneration. How often have I cried, "What does it take?
What?"

After more than ten years of observing the testimony of
God's transforming power and love in my own life, my
mother is still not a believer. Her son, who used to smoke,
curse, and chase women, is now a new kind of man, a new
spirit, who lives to serve the God of our fathers. She stops
her ears, closes her eyes, refuses to understand the
implications of these changes, and is more concerned about
what the neighbors might say. She has heard enough about
"this Jesus thing," and has lived so long she's just trying to
make it to the finish line with out any more controversy.
What does it take to bring such a one repentantly before
Israel's God?

And it came to pass after these things, that the
son of the woman, the mistress of the house, fell
sick; and his sickness was so sore, that there was
no breath left in him.

1 Kings 17:17

Nothing less than the death of her son could have brought
that Zidonian widow woman to the necessary brokenness
that precedes real contrition. She had nothing left that
mattered to her but one son, and he was more dear to her

62

than her own life. When God took her son's life, the stone walls of that mother's heart were smashed and the light of the Spirit shone in:

> And she said unto Elijah, What have I to do with thee, O thou man of God? *art thou come unto me to call my sin to remembrance, and to slay my son?*
>
> 1 Kings 17:18
> (our italics)

This woman was certainly no great scholar, but somehow she understood that the abrupt taking of her son was directly and intimately related to her own spiritual condition before God. "Art thou come unto me to call *my* sin to remembrance?" Would to God that the more tutored people might equally understand that the dealings we receive at His hand have to do with unconfessed sin and a consequent separation from a loving Father.

> Or despisest thou the riches of his goodness and forbearance and longsuffering; not knowing that *the goodness of God leadeth thee to repentance?*
>
> Romans 2:4
> (our italics)

Many may inquire, "Is it *good* to take a woman's only son?" The answer must be "*Yes*, if it will save a soul from eternal burning." Wherever people are vulnerable, *there* will God touch them. If a man is indifferent about his own life and is ready to go to hell, then God may put His finger on the person or thing which is more precious than himself. The Lord is ". . . not willing that any should perish, but that all should come to repentance" (2 Peter 3:9b).

Like Joseph on many occasions before him, this prophet found himself surprised by a critical situation of which he had neither forewarning nor explanation from God. Again, crisis revealed the true mettle of a man. The same touchstone shall be used increasingly at the end of the ages. Elijah, joined to the Lord and one spirit with Him, acted instantly:

> And he said unto her, Give me thy son. And he took him out of her bosom, and carried him up into a loft, where he abode, and laid him upon his own bed.
>
> And he cried unto the Lord, and said, O Lord my God, hast thou also brought evil upon the widow with whom I sojourn, by slaying her son?
>
> And he stretched himself upon the child three times, and cried unto the Lord, and said, O Lord my God, I pray thee, let this child's soul come into him again.
>
> And the Lord heard the voice of Elijah; and the soul of the child came into him again, and he revived.
>
> 1 Kings 17:19-22

We see here *not* simply an interesting historical narrative of one man's reaction to an unexpected and untoward circumstance; in Elijah's response, God is showing us *today* the definitive pattern of His end-time evangelism. He is calling us to the corpse of a dead world. We have hoped that we could save it with bumper stickers, literature campaigns, "Christian" pop music, and countless other human programs, all without a modicum of embarrassment. "No stoop, no fuss, no bother."

This world shall be saved only by the willingness of men

and women to take the stiff, cold, icky cadaver of the world up to their abode, *where their own bed is,* and stretch it out on their satiny-smooth sheets. "Oh, Art, listen, I was willing to come to the conferences and the potluck dinners, but my bed is my own private domain." EXACTLY. There is no shortcut: if we are not willing to have that privacy penetrated by a holy burden and concern for the world, we shall play no active part in its revival.

Stretched out upon that corpse, fingertip to fingertip, eyeball to eyeball, and jowl to jowl, the prophet cried to the Lord three times, "Let breath come back to this dead child." Elijah, seen and heard only by God, was moving in the same Spirit as Moses, when he interceded for a spiritually dead Israel:

> Yet now, if thou wilt forgive their sin—; and if not, blot me, I pray thee, out of thy book which thou hast written.
>
> Exodus 32:32

It is the same attitude that Paul expressed as he spoke from his heart about his Jewish people:

> For I could wish that myself were accursed from Christ for my brethren, my kinsmen according to the flesh.
>
> Who are Israelites; to whom pertaineth the adoption, and the glory, and the covenants, and the giving of the law, and the service of God, and the promises;
>
> Whose are the fathers, and of whom as concerning the flesh Christ came, who is over all, God blessed for ever. Amen.
>
> Romans 9:3-5

David's son Absalom was slain while attempting to overthrow his father's kingdom. When the king heard of the death, he did not rejoice over the death of an enemy:

> And the king was much moved, and went up to the chamber over the gate, and wept: and as he went, thus he said, O my son Absalom, my son, my son Absalom! would God I had died for thee, O Absalom, my son, my son!
>
> 2 Samuel 18:33

In all of these lives, we see the love of Christ shed abroad in men's hearts by the Holy Spirit. From the mouth of Elijah God heard the cries of a man after His own heart. In that moment, that prophet's whole body, pressed against the dead boy, became a living prayer: "O Lord my God, take the breath which is in me, take the *life* which is in me, and put it within this child."

The spirit of the world has permeated and corrupted the attitudes of the Body of Christ. We have taken upon ourselves business mentalities, and have thought that, through devices, stratagems, and programs, we could save a world. There can never be life without, first, a willingness to suffer death. It is the cardinal principle of God, and is inseparable from the central meaning of His cross. "So then death worketh in us," Paul said, "but life in you" (2 Corinthians 4:12). There has got to be a readiness to prostrate ourselves out over a dead world—in all of its clammy cold stiffness—and, as our sheets get soiled, cry out of the kishkes, out of the gut, three times or three hundred times, "Lord, let him live!"

> And Elijah took the child, and brought him down out of the chamber into the house, and

delivered him unto his mother: and Elijah said, *See, thy son liveth.*

1 Kings 17:23
(our italics)

Shall anything less suffice? The world has heard all of our slogans, our clever little sayings, and it is still unmoved. It shall take more than words to pierce through the rigid walls of their hearts; they are longing unknowingly for a demonstration of the resurrection life of God. "For the kingdom of God is not in word, but in power" (1 Corinthians 4:20).

I know several Jewish families who have already come into the kingdom in such a way as this. A friend of mine, a Jewish executive in Los Angeles, had a fifteen-year-old son who was a hopeless heroin addict. This wealthy family had sent him to the best doctors, specialists, psychiatrists, institutions, you name it—it all availed nothing. One day, by the grace of God, that kid staggered, more dead than alive, into a Teen Challenge center. The love of his *Masheach*, fully alive in those people, welcomed him in. He got saved there and filled with the Spirit of the Holy One of Israel.

When the workers brought the son back to his family, they beheld one who had been brought back from the dead. *See, thy son liveth.* The father, who formerly had not even been able to mention the name Jesus, got saved shortly after, and then the mother, brother, and sister. Because there were some believers who were willing to impart the divine breath which was in them into a lifeless boy, there is an entire family going on with God today that is a collective praise unto the mercies of the Almighty.

The Word in Thy Mouth

And the woman said to Elijah, Now by this I

know that thou art a man of God, and that the word of the Lord in thy mouth is truth.

1 Kings 17:24

"That other stuff was impressive. I really enjoyed the barrel of meal not wasting and the cruse of oil not failing; but now by *this*, life where there was death in my dear son, I know that you are God's man, and in *your* mouth His word is truth." I used to believe that the word of God in our mouths is *always* truth. How can we believe that if we parrot the correct words we are somehow expressing the truth of the Lord? In many of our mouths, these pronouncements amount to hardly more than a religious belch.

As a young believer, there was a phenomenon that would really baffle me. I could hear a certain message preached ten times (how many new messages are there?), and nine times out of ten I would be left completely unimpressed. I would leave the room, the words already forgotten, and my thoughts would cluster around such issues as, "Where am I gonna eat?" Then the tenth man would arrive and speak the same essential message, right out of the same text, and POW!—something would be loosed in my heart. I might not sleep much that night; and weeks, months, years later, that word would still be reverberating in my inner man. My attitudes, perceptions, speech, and conduct, my *life*, had been changed.

Life had gone forth from that speaker because the word of the Lord in *his* mouth was truth. I don't think that it became truth in him because he diligently did his Bible studies, knew how to use a concordance, was pretty sharp in speaking, and knew how to quote the right Scriptures and subscribe to the correct doctrines. There is no cheap, easy, or coldly mechanical way to become a fit vessel for eternal truth. There was more than a Bible study going on that day; there

68

was a man who was dead and hid with Christ standing before God and God's people, and the same Spirit Who raised that widow woman's son was freely pouring the waters of life into my own thirsty soul.

> For our gospel came not unto you in word only, but also in power, and in the Holy Ghost, and in much assurance; as ye know what manner of men we were among you for your sake.
>
> 1 Thessalonians 1:5

Art Thou He That Troubleth Israel?

> And it came to pass after many days, that the word of the Lord came to Elijah in the third year, saying, Go, shew thyself unto Ahab; and I will send rain upon the earth.
>
> 1 Kings 18:1

Once again, Elijah was directed by the Lord to walk towards what appeared to be certain destruction. The prophet knew nothing of what might intervene between his initial reunion with the king and the falling of the famine-ending rain. What did such a man do?

> And Elijah went to shew himself unto Ahab. And there was a sore famine in Samaria.
>
> 1 Kings 18:2

The reception given to this man who lived to bring the love and truth of God to his backslidden people is the same one that Jesus received and is the one that we can expect:

> And it came to pass, when Ahab saw Elijah,

that Ahab said unto him, *Art thou he that troubleth Israel?*
1 Kings 18:17
(our italics)

We shall not be applauded for our fidelity to God, but shall receive from the world the same reward given Joseph, Elijah, and our Lord Himself: reproach and false accusation. As God's concern for the Jews is manifested in our lives, we shall be met with rigid resistance not only from rabbis, but also from "Christian" ministers: "Art thou he that troubleth Israel? Why don't you leave them alone? Haven't they suffered enough?"

One rabbi said:

> We call on the Christian conscience to recognize that a Christian theology based on the negation of Judaism and that sees Christianity as a substitution for the Jewish faith, will seriously impact upon the existence of the Jewish people. After the Nazi holocaust, which destroyed one-third of the Jewish people, and in face of Soviet threats to carry out a program of enforced cultural and religious assimilation which could destroy another one-third of the Jewish people, the whole question of ethics to convert the Jewish people out of their religion becomes a morally unconscionable position.
>
> Rabbi Mark H. Tannenbaum
> National Director of Inter-religious Affairs Department of the American Jewish Committee
> *L.A. Herald Examiner,*
> January 27, 1973

That's what I call a statement. What rhetoric! Every word is like a cannon blast. The accusation is a heavy one, and has blown more than one Christian out of the arena. If, after we have stopped trembling, we examine the content of the charge, we quickly discover that it is based upon a foundation of self-righteousness; we must ask in return, "does the position attacked here have anything to do with real Christianity?" God forbid! Did Elijah want to seriously impact upon the existence of the Jews and turn them away from the God of Abraham, Isaac, Jacob and Moses? Did Jesus? He said:

> Think not that I am come to destroy the law, or the prophets: I am not come to destroy, but to fulfill.
>
> Matthew 5:17

At the bidding of the Spirit, I have shared the gospel of our Messiah with many of my Jewish people. Some have believed unto life, and we have joyously embraced as newly found brothers and sisters. More than once, however, I have heard, "You're worse than Hitler. You're a greater menace to us, Katz, than he was; he only tried to destroy our bodies, but you're trying to steal our souls." The darts of accusation don't stop at Art Katz, but always continue toward their ultimate target, the crucified and risen *Masheach*. It is the Light of the world Who is being rejected by those who choose darkness.

There is today much schmaltzy, sentimental talk of love for the Jewish people, and there are many who are nobly demonstrating palpitations for Israel. "Oh, I love the Jews. When I visited Israel, I just fell madly in love with those people. I even give a little something each year to plant trees in the Holy Land." What about the Israel right under your

71

nose? Will you shout, "Why don't you leave them alone?" when the words of eternal life are offered to them by the mouths of both Gentile and Jewish believers?

When the oil crisis reaches its full scope, we shall suddenly see a refreshing breakthrough of reality upon the gamesmanship of this world. Don't be surprised if you see bumper stickers that say, "Oil yes, Jews no." That crisis shall be only one of the means that God shall use to separate the sheep from the goats. There is going to be only one body of people who shall love Israel and the Jewish people, and it shall be for a reason which has nothing to do with nice human sentiment. It has everything to do with the *Ruach Hakodesh*, Who indwells and watches over His flock.

In *Ben Israel*, I wrote about my dear friends in northern California; I have rarely seen as pure and strong a love for the Jewish people as that which flows through those Gentiles (if I can use that word for men and women who have come to the knowledge of God). I asked my hostess, Mama Fultz, one day, why she and her family love the Jews so much and have such a love for Israel. Her answer bears much repetition, for I have never heard a more perfect one. She said, "I don't know why. All I know is that our God loves the children of Israel, and to the degree that we have His love in us, we love you also."

On one of my visits to that old farmhouse, I brought my mother along with me. On that particular occasion, she was hopping mad. It was Mother's Day and I was scheduled to speak at a church. That's my timing. She was determined to sit outside in the car and watch the baby while I went into the church. Church. Is there a word more distasteful to Jews? Yecch. How icky can you get?

By some kind of miracle, she eventually got out of the car and wandered into that building. What a wipe-out: booming out of the organ and out of the mouths of the congregation were *Havenu Shalom Alechem* and *Heenay Mah Tov Oomah Nayim*. My mother volunteered to sing one of those songs, and about halfway through she faltered, having forgotten the lyrics. My good friend Alberta, Gentile believer, who was playing the organ, helped her with the Hebrew words. At the end of that day, my mother said to me, "I have never been so loved in all my life." She had tasted the sweetness of the Spirit.

In twelve years, I have not been able to adequately convey to my mother, who is a very clever woman, the difference between a so-called Christian and a born-again believer who is filled with and moved by the Spirit of Israel's God. She can understand many esoteric things, but she cannot fathom this. I have said, "Mom, not everybody who's a Christian is a Christian. Not all Israel is Israel. There are a lot of goyim who sit in pews who are as removed from God as our own people, but there are those who are born again by the *Ruach*, true believers." When the day comes in which the Jews shall experience, in this country and throughout the world, non-Jewish believers standing with them in persecution perhaps greater in magnitude than what we suffered in Germany, my mother and my kinsmen will see at last this crucial distinction.

A woman told me about a strange dream that she had, a nightmare prophetic in its implications. In it, her family was sleeping in a large house, when suddenly there was a furious pounding on the front door. Everybody put on their bathrobes, gathered together downstairs, and opened the door. Hooded men rushed in and commanded them to get dressed. The family was told they could not take anything with them, but had to evacuate the house immediately. They were tossed into the back seats of various cars which drove off into the night. That woman, in her panic, said to her abductors, "Why are you doing this?" The answer she received was, "You are among those who love the Jews."

During a recent visit to Germany, I spoke with many Germans who had lived in that country during the Third Reich. They were "Christians" by label, but, in truth, their lives were not under the loving dominion of Christ. I asked them, "What did you do when you looked out of the window in the early 1930s and you saw the Jewish kids being beaten up, the old men having their beards pulled, the store windows being smashed, and the filthy epithets being scrawled over the sidewalks? What did you do?" They said, "We pulled the shade down, and we walked away."

In the hour of tribulation, some of the chosen people of God, in the natural and in the spiritual, are going to find each other. Those Jewish people shall know who their allies are, and will learn that the Holy One of Israel has not forgotten them. Great love shall be born in the midst of this work of salvation and deliverance, but, at the same time, every servant of God must be prepared to receive, even while his hand is extended, the rebuke of Ahab: "Art thou he that troubleth Israel?"

The Confrontation

Elijah did not skulk away into the shadows like the proverbial dog with his tail between his legs.

> And he answered, I have not troubled Israel; but thou, and thy father's house, in that ye have forsaken the commandments of the Lord, and thou has followed Baalim.
>
> 1 Kings 18:18

He did not mince words, but straightway delivered the undiluted truth of God to the evil king. The same Spirit Who enabled Elijah to stand with boldness before Ahab shall

74

sustain men and women in the face of fierce reproach and persecution at the end of the ages. Jesus said:

> Behold, I send you forth as sheep in the midst of wolves: be ye therefore wise as serpents, and harmless as doves.
>
> But beware of men: for they will deliver you up to the councils, and they will scourge you in their synagogues;
>
> And ye shall be brought before governors and kings for my sake, for a testimony against them and the Gentiles.
>
> But when they deliver you up, *take no thought how or what ye shall speak: for it shall be given you in that same hour what ye shall speak.*
>
> *For it is not ye that speak, but the Spirit of your Father which speaketh in you.*
>
> Matthew 10:16-20
(our italics)

We need never be on the defensive. God shall sometimes require us to be silent, and He shall at times bid us to speak, but *always* He will keep us firmly planted in the safety of His unconquerable truth. I have been accused by many people of troubling Israel. The love of God has demanded each time that I either keep my mouth shut or unreservedly proclaim the uncompromised truth of God: "It is not I who trouble Israel. *You*, you officials of the Jewish community who have kept from that community the knowledge of the living Messiah, *you* who have made the New Testament (and many sections of the Old Testament) out of bounds and taboo, *you* who have not allowed Jewish believers to give our witness and have attempted to cut us off from any effectual contact with our own people, *you* have led them to follow false gods, not I."

Elijah went even further:

> Now therefore send, and gather to me all Israel unto mount Carmel, and the prophets of Baal four hundred and fifty, and the prophets of the groves four hundred, which eat at Jezebel's table.
>
> So Ahab sent unto the children of Israel, and gathered the prophets together unto mount Carmel.
>
> 1 Kings 18:19, 20

Only the authority of God could have commanded that apostate king to fulfill those enormous conditions. Without the presence of the Spirit empowering him, Elijah would have come off as just another pathetic, power-hungry crank.

> And Elijah came unto all the people, and said, How long halt ye between two opinions? if the Lord be God, follow him: but if Baal, then follow him. And the people answered him not a word.
>
> 1 Kings 18:21

I can picture their stricken faces as they gazed upon that hairy guy in his leather girdle, speaking with absolute authority. Their mouths were stopped. The sharp sword of the Spirit deeply pierced their hearts, as that wilderness prophet put forth the challenge of the Lord. "How long shall you continue in your cop-out religiosity? How long shall you continue to play at your outward game of so-called Judaism when in your hearts, like pagans, you have gone whoring after other gods? If God be God, follow Him. Put up or shut up." There was no answer.

Then said Elijah unto the people, I, even I only, remain a prophet of the Lord; but Baal's prophets are four hundred and fifty men.

Let them therefore give us two bullocks; and let them choose one bullock for themselves, and cut it in pieces, and lay it on wood, and put no fire under: and I will dress the other bullock, and lay it on wood, and put no fire under:

And call ye on the name of your gods, and I will call on the name of the Lord: and the God that answereth by fire, let him be God. And all the people answered and said, It is well spoken.

1 Kings 18:22-24

To this the people could answer, "Hey, that's good, we like that part;" that faithless crowd never expected for a moment that there was going to be an answer from Heaven. They probably thought something like, "We'll get rid of this *mishoogenah*, this nudnik, this eccentric nuisance. Certainly no one can fulfill these impossible conditions." That prophet, shaped by God's hand, knew just as well as his adversaries that his number would be up if the fire did not fall! Confrontations and showdowns of no lesser magnitude shall mark these last days for every believer who is walking in the narrow way.

We have a living God Who answers by fire. I once attended a conference to which a rabbi had also been invited. We had both been asked to speak to an assembly of several hundred people. When we first saw each other, we must have looked like two cats with their backs arched and their hair standing straight up. He could not stand the sight of me—I just turned his guts sour.

He gave his presentation first. It was letter perfect, cool, intellectual, and polished, but utterly lifeless. The "God" he spoke of was an impersonal fabrication of the human mind, not the Almighty One Who brought the Israelites out of Egypt.

My heart was pounding and I was sweating profusely as I listened to yet another religious leader propound the perspective which has blinded my people for centuries. I leaned over, and as my eye fell on him, I said, "You make your sacrifice and call upon the name of your God, and I'll make my sacrifice and call upon the God of my fathers, and let God be God Who answers by fire."

That learned fellow gulped and said, "What do you mean?"

I answered, "I'm sick of the kind of talk that I hear from ministers of your kind, both rabbis and other clergymen, speaking about God as an impersonal force in the universe, some distant and higher power somewhere, some concept. I tell you, I may not be too bright, but I know that any concept has its origin in a man's skull, and anything that a man can think and devise is less than what God is. No concept is ever going to answer with fire from Heaven."

"What kind of fire are you talking about?" he asked.

"I speak of the fire that can set an alcoholic free, reconcile a marriage, deliver a drug addict, or heal a cancer. When was the last time you saw that kind of fire fall in your temple? My God answers by fire."

There was no rejoinder.

Every confrontation that the sons and daughters of God shall have with the children of this world shall have, as its basic blueprint, the same conditions that were presented by Elijah: "You call on the name of your gods, and I'll call upon the name of the Lord." In that moment, you can be sure that our calling upon His name shall be more than the verbal equivalent of rubbing on a magic lamp. To call upon the name of the Lord is more than saying "in the name of Jesus" as some kind of magical incantation, more than mimicking the right words. Elijah was a man who *knew* his God. He was not relying upon an easy formula. Meaningfully calling upon God's name is an intimately personal expression of a relationship that is longstanding and deep in an act occasioned by God in keeping with His character and way.

> And Elijah said unto the prophets of Baal, Choose you one bullock for youselves, and dress it first; for ye are many; and call on the name of your gods, but put no fire under.
> And they took the bullock which was given them, and they dressed it, and called on the name of Baal from morning even until noon, saying, O Baal, hear us. But there was no voice, nor any that answered. And they leaped upon the altar which was made.
>
> 1 Kings 18:25, 26

Those people were sincere religionists who were hoping for an answer from the "higher power" that they believed they had plugged into. "But," in the critical hour of confrontation, "there was no voice, nor any that answered." My heart winces every time I read that line because I know there are countless thousands of people who, in the crucial juncture of their lives, shall call upon their imaginary gods and receive no answer.

I fear that, in that day, my own mother may call upon the "God" that she thinks she is following and find out that, after all, it was only *Yiddishkeit:* matzoh balls, gefilte fish, Israel bonds, and a whole welter and confusion of things which she has equated with God. My prayer is that she will see and acknowledge the truth that she, in fact, does not know Him, because she has forsaken His Son.

> Jesus saith unto him, I am the way, the truth, and the life: no man cometh unto the Father, but by me.
>
> John 14:6

> All things are delivered unto me of my Father: and no man knoweth the Son, but the Father; neither knoweth any man the Father, save the Son, and he to whomsoever the Son will reveal him.
>
> Matthew 11:27

Those men leaped upon the altar in their frenzy. What a characteristic picture of every kind of false religion. Even "true" religion that is no longer divinely vital, although the correct terminologies are employed, will, before long, be characterized by a vacuous leaping upon altars. There will be lots of jumping, lots of noise, lots of activities, lots of abracadabra, lots of "charismatic" nonsense *to fill the silences* in the hope that the excitement which we have created can pass for the presence of the Holy Spirit. But God has counseled us, "Be still, and know that I am God" (Psalm 46:10a).

Mockery in the Service of God

> And it came to pass at noon, that Elijah mocked them, and said, Cry aloud: for he is a god; either he is talking, or he is pursuing, or he is in a journey, or peradventure he sleepeth, and must be awaked.
>
> 1 Kings 18:27

The King James Version is very polite: the phrase "he is pursuing" more directly and unashamedly translated would read "he is sitting on a toilet." That's not very genteel, but God has spoken and will speak such things to challenge people when the issue is life and death. God is looking for those who will not flinch from lending Him their mouths for such foolish speaking.

Many dutiful churchmen might object, "God would never have a respectable Christian act in that manner." I am not as quick as I used to be to say what God will do and what He will not do. I have heard some things come out of my mouth that I would never, of my own choosing, have spoken.

One night, I was scheduled to speak at a Pentecostal church in a certain American city, and I arrived in that town in my usual condition—wasted, exhausted, empty. I went up to the platform and felt utterly drained of anything to say to those people. What a congregation! I had never seen a more healthy-looking group. After the choir had sung a few songs, the pastor gave me an introduction that was so glib and polished that I began to wonder if it was really me who was being described.

He went on and on, and the more lofty the rhetoric got the more my heart sank. Somehow, in the course of that presentation, I realized that, at some point in his life, that minister had passed from being an honest man of God to being a slick professional, and he had not even been aware that he had crossed an invisible boundary line between the two. At the conclusion of his remarks, he said, "Now the choir will sing one more song, and then Brother Katz will minister to us." I thought, "Oh my God, I have nothing to say. I need more to sit at *their* feet and be ministered to by them."

Then the choir sang their last song. With a syrupy

sweetness, they belted out a nursery-school melody: "I need Jesus, you need Jesus, we need Jesus. . . ." As those beaming faces continued to sing, my heart was sinking lower and lower with every stanza. If you choose to be like Elijah, there will be times when you shall feel quite freaky; you are going to have strange sensations when everybody else seems to be having a ball, and God is going to give you peculiar signals that no one else is experiencing. In my heart of hearts, I was becoming increasingly depressed, though every outward sign seemed in contradiction to my inner state. All the physical eye and ear could perceive was a glowingly healthy congregation and a choir singing in great praise to God.

The song concluded, the singers filed out of the choir loft and took their seats, and everybody was waiting expectantly. Many had their tape recorder microphones poised to catch the jewels that were about to fall from my lips. I got up and dragged my carcass to the pulpit. What I then heard coming out of my mouth, in a terribly mocking tone, was, "I need Jee-zus, you need Jee-zus, we need Jee-zus. . . ." I clapped my hand over my mouth and thought, "I've gone off the deep end now. It's finally happened."

I profusely apologized for my failure to pray before I spoke. I prayed out loud, "Lord, forgive me, cleanse me, possess me, use my mouth to speak to this congregation. I'm sorry I blew it. Take over and discharge the burden of Your heart. In Jesus' holy name. *Amen.*" I opened my mouth again, and what came out was, "I need Jee-zus, you need Jee-zus, we need Jee-zus. . . ." That singsong mockery was followed by three simple words, "Really? What for?" The sword of God went right into the kishkes.

That congregation had thought themselves rich, but God

stripped them and showed them their nakedness. That service went on until one o'clock in the morning, and the pastor was stretched out like a dead man, face down on the platform, for two hours. When he got up, he had a new face: he had passed from death to life.

One of the elders of the church, who was going to give his testimony at a Christian businessmen's meeting that week, took the microphone and confessed that he was in a continual state of adultery. That was only the beginning of a deluge of confessions that poured forth from that innocent-looking congregation. Here was the living testimony of the truth of Jesus' words, "Now do ye Pharisees make clean the outside of the cup and the platter; but your inward part is full of ravening and wickedness" (Luke 11:39). Following hard upon the heels of those confessions came the healing and delivering work of the Spirit.

The wife of the man who had been in adultery had a busted kneecap, and she timidly asked me to come over and pray for her. I told her to place both her hands on her knee, and I put my hand on hers and prayed for healing. I began to walk away and noticed that she still had that dismayed, stricken look on her face. I said, "Dear woman, why don't you believe God and praise Him? It's when Israel praised God in the beauty of God's holiness that He gave answer."

The Spirit was crying out for the reappearance of the attitude of a Job, who, in the midst of the catastrophe that his life had become, did not charge God foolishly, and could affirm, "Though he slay me, yet will I trust in him" (Job 13:15a). I had no time for a self-pitying immaturity in a woman who had probably been a believer for forty years. As I was leaving her, I said, "Go down on that concrete floor and praise God." Amazingly enough, she did it. It was an act done in spirit and in truth, an expression of loving worship which was not contingent upon any manifestation of healing. This was no quickie success formula, but a simple, unconditional praise from the heart to her living God. At the moment that her knee touched the floor and her hands were lifted above her head, she was healed.

God did a great work in that place, and it began when he mocked His own people. I have learned to respect the variety of the Lord's dealings. The spontaneous, creative workings of the Spirit are entirely free of any of the preconceived notions we have developed in the light of our past experience. He is doing a new thing in the earth and will not be bound by human conventions.

The Restoration of God's Altar

And they cried aloud, and cut themselves after their manner with knives and lancets, till the blood gushed out upon them.

And it came to pass, when midday was past, and they prophesied until the time of the offering of the evening sacrifice, that *there was neither voice, nor any to answer, nor any that regarded.*

1 Kings 18:28, 29
(our italics)

These tragic souls tried every kind of fleshly device they could think of. The very act of shedding their own blood is a grotesque parody of God's ordained way of salvation through substitutionary atonement: we are presented here with a perfect tableau of the futility of men's efforts to save themselves. Intellectualizations and tin gods shall never provide the fire of deliverance.

I visited Yugoslavia during the winter of 1975, and had one of the more melancholy experiences of my life there. In the midst of a nondescript Serbian town, an abandoned synagogue remains. With its plaster falling off and many of its bricks loose, it is like an old, broken-down, and empty box. My heart broke as I gazed upon that forsaken building, and I recalled the words that the Lord had spoken to a people who refused to recognize Him:

O Jerusalem, Jerusalem, thou that killest the prophets, and stonest them which are sent unto thee, how often would I have gathered thy children together, even as a hen gathereth her chickens under her wings, and ye would not!
Behold, your house is left unto you desolate.
For I say unto you, Ye shall not see me henceforth, till ye shall say, Blessed is he that cometh in the name of the Lord.

Matthew 23:37-39
(our italics)

In that Yugoslavian community, there was just a handful of Jews who had survived the last holocaust. In the moment of crisis, the religious traditions of men could not save what had been a flourishing community of thousands. "There was neither voice, nor any to answer, nor any that regarded." The love of God is calling and preparing men and women who shall challenge the false gods of our generation, and say to a backslidden people, "How long will you halt between two opinions? If the Lord be God, follow Him."

And Elijah said unto all the people, Come near unto me. And all the people came near unto him. And he repaired the altar of the Lord that was broken down.

And Elijah took twelve stones, according to the number of the tribes of the sons of Jacob, unto whom the word of the Lord came, saying, Israel shall be thy name:

And with the stones he built an altar in the name of the Lord. . . .

1 Kings 18:30-32a

One of the first functions of the prophet is to restore the altar that is fallen, to re-establish the purity and the holiness of God's house. The emphasis of the Spirit upon this specific ministry shall increase as we approach this world's final hour. It is painful to witness the phoney worship, counterfeit religiosity, fleshly flamboyance, noise, public relations ballyhoo, and all the other jive that goes on in many churches in the name of the Lord. God's altars need to be restored, and this work needs to start with the invisible altars in our hearts. People have got to be brought back to the knowledge that God is *holy*.

. . . and he made a trench about the altar, as great as would contain two measures of seed.

And he put the wood in order, and cut the bullock in pieces, and laid him on the wood, and said, Fill four barrels with water, and pour it on the burnt sacrifice, and on the wood.

And he said, Do it the second time. And they did it the second time. And he said, Do it the third time. And they did it the third time.

And the water ran round about the altar; and he filled the trench also with water.

1 Kings 18:32b-35

When I read this passage for the first time, my heart was

86

beating fast, and I thought, "What kind of *mishegass* (nonsense) is this? This is crazy. Take it easy, fella. Isn't it enough to believe God to consume a *dry* sacrifice with fire? What are you saturating it with water for? That's no way to prepare an altar. Are you trying to test God?"

I understand now, however, that there is a principle here that God's children in the end times must see. Our sacrifices have been altogether too dry. There shall be no heavenly fire without a sacrifice in which the flesh is cut up, laid out, and saturated, twelve barrels full, with the repentant tears of God's people.

Basilea Schlink says in one of her books that the cancer of modern Christianity is our lovelessness. Oh, I know we have lots of back slaps, bear hugs, embraces and handshakes of all kinds, but the kind of love which is sacrificial at its core is not much in evidence. We need to ask God's forgiveness for our glib phrases about saving the world, and for our delight in those activities which we called "witnessing," which are too often compensatory devices for carnal living.

It is one thing to kneel and piously say the right things and say that we have concern for a lost world, but it is quite something else to *break* and *weep* and respond to deep calling unto deep in a profound bond with our Creator. James tells us that it is the effectual *fervent* prayer of righteous men and women that avails much (James 5:16b). It is this kind of burden-bearing that shall overcome at the restored altar.

Shortly after my return to California from Jerusalem where I had just found the Lord, I gave my first testimony at a little church in my community. A little roly-poly woman came up to me after the service. "Brother Katz," she said (it was strange to hear a woman say "Brother Katz"), "you don't know me, but my daughter was a student of yours in high school. She knew that you were an atheist and a radical, and she would come home in the afternoons weeping over you. Since the first time that happened, she and I have been praying for you."

Something exploded in my heart, and my words to her must have sounded like a needle that was stuck on a record: "So you're the one, so you're the one, so you're the one whose prayers have entered me into the Kingdom of God." God had not responded to schmaltzy sentiment or to drummed-up emotions; He had heard the fervent cry that was born in His own heart come through righteous instruments who had become one spirit with Him. Fire fell upon the tear-drenched altar and an unsuspecting atheist fell before the God of his fathers crying "The Lord, He is God! The Lord, He is God!"

This Day

And it came to pass at the time of the offering of the evening sacrifice, that Elijah the prophet came near, and said, Lord God of Abraham, Isaac, and of Israel, let it be known this day that thou art God in Israel, and that I am thy servant, and that I have done all these things at thy word.

1 Kings 18:36

There is no mention here of God explicitly speaking to the prophet about how to set up the altar, and yet Elijah said to the Lord that he had done everything *at thy word*. The structure that he stood before was not the fruit of human cleverness. This was a man so possessed of the living God that the One to Whom he was joined could lead him step by step in the establishing of that altar.

The stage was set for the glory of God to be revealed, and God's servant knew that the moment had arrived. "Let it be known *this day*. . . ." Such moments shall come in each of our lives, moments of confrontation, moments of eternal consequence. Our Lord does not consider it wasteful to spend a long time in the preparation of a man, in order that, in that crucial moment, there shall be answer.

Can you imagine the agony and impatience that Elijah must have felt as he watched the systematic annihilation of all of God's prophets, and saw, day by day, the disintegrating and degenerating of the moral condition of the people of Israel? He never once ventured to come onto the stage by his own volition. He never once said, "I can't take it any more. I've got to speak. I can't be silent." In discipline he was hidden and obscure until the moment of God's choosing, and then he perfectly performed the thing for which God had shaped his life.

Are you willing to be dead and hid with God in Christ until His glory shall be revealed? There is no itch stronger than the one that young people have: they long to do, to be seen, to perform, to be rewarded, to be acknowledged. To each one who is impatient to be recognized, God would counsel, "Wait! It's easy for you to distribute tracts; it's easy for you to knock on doors; it's easy for you to witness; but I have some other thing that has a much higher priority—My dealing with you in the depths of your inner man, where no one can see you, perfecting your character, that I might bring you forth in the perfect moment, wholly tested and wholly mine."

Elijah cried out:

> Hear me, O Lord, hear me, that this people may know that thou art the Lord God, and that *thou hast turned their heart back again.*
>
> 1 Kings 18:37
> (our italics)

The same prophet who had lain before the Lord in supplication for that widow woman's son was now interceding for all Israel. He sought no position or fame for himself, but asked only that his perishing people might see God's glory and, in true repentance, be saved. God hears such prayers:

> Then the fire of the Lord fell, and consumed the burnt sacrifice, and the wood, and the stones, and the dust, and licked up the water that was in the trench.
> And when all the people saw it, they fell on their faces: and they said, The Lord, he is the God; the Lord, he is the God.
>
> 1 Kings 18:38, 39

God's answer is always worth waiting for. Whenever we impatiently attempt to fulfill the intentions of God by fleshly means, we always wind up with an unblessed end. Abraham, in his hotness to bring into existence the child that God had promised him, copulated with Hagar, his wife's Egyptian handmaid, and reaped Ishmael. Isaac, the child of promise, eventually was miraculously born from Sarah's old and barren womb, but there could be no undoing of the earlier hasty act; the seed of Ishmael has been a thorn in Israel's side unto this very day.

Our human enthusiasm shall never be enough to bring a world to real contrition before God. If we wait upon the Lord, He shall prepare us to be men and women who can invoke His holy fire. Our premature, nervous activity will never be of any avail, and will only wear us down.

But they that wait upon the Lord shall renew

their strength; they shall mount up with wings as eagles; they shall run, and not be weary; and they shall walk, and not faint.

Isaiah 40:31

Fire

It is only when the fire falls, when the Holy Spirit sovereignly transforms a situation, consuming everything that can burn, that cities and nations shall fall on their faces and proclaim, "The Lord, He is God." Before we can hope to invoke the kind of fire from heaven that shall turn the hearts of men and women back to the Lord, a preliminary blaze must occur within our individual lives. Every fleshly quality of God's people must be cut and laid bare at the altar of the Spirit: our pride, fear, ambition, selfishness, lust, all of it must be offered as a sacrifice wet with tears and ready for the burning.

I am not a pyromaniac, but I am convinced that the remainder of mankind's time on this earth shall be marked by one kind of fire or another. In the time of Noah, God judged the whole earth with floods of water, "but," Peter tells us,

the heavens and the earth, which are now, by the same word are kept in store, reserved unto fire against the day of judgment and perdition of ungodly men.

2 Peter 3:7

Elie Wiesel, the great Jewish writer, in his book called *Night*, depicts the final stages of the Nazi holocaust in central Europe. Although the author is not a believer himself, the Lord has much to teach us through his

91

straightforward account of real events. Wiesel's own family was stripped from him and murdered in that demonic rampage. They lived in the little town of Sighet in Transylvania, and, in the beginning of the book, everything on the surface of life seemed peaceful enough. All was "business as usual."

Entire Jewish communities in Poland, Germany, Austria, and other places had already been obliterated, but that little hamlet, couched in apparent security up in the mountains, had not yet been touched. Everybody assured each other that this too would pass and would never extend far enough to touch them. Jewish people are inveterate optimists; we have faith in everything—except in God and His *Masheach* Jesus.

As a young boy, the author had studied and practiced the cabbala, the ancient Jewish mystical system whose teachings run counter to God's commandments in the Scriptures. One day, all foreign Jews were expelled from Sighet, and among them was Wiesel's eccentric mentor of those forbidden arts, Moche the beadle. He had been taken captive by the Gestapo, and in the forest of Galicia, in Poland, had witnessed the unchecked evil of the oppressors. After being wounded in the leg, he was left for dead, and, miraculously, escaped and returned to Sighet.

He spoke to everyone of what he had seen. He was a different man. No longer did he winsomely share his cabbalistic God-concepts with his old friends who had used to listen so eagerly; no longer did he sing. His eyes had been opened to the mystery of iniquity, and he could only warn everybody of the coming peril.

People refused not only to believe his stories, but even to listen to them.

"He's just trying to make us pity him. What an imagination he has!" they said. Or even: "Poor fellow. He's gone mad."

And as for Moche, he wept.[1]

The young boy pitied him, and asked that outcast a question that every believer can expect:

"Why are you so anxious that people should believe what you say. In your place, I shouldn't care whether they believed me or not. . . ."

He closed his eyes, as though to escape time.

"You don't understand," he said in despair. "You can't understand. I have been saved miraculously. I managed to get back here. Where did I get the strength from? I wanted to come back to Sighet to tell you the story of my death. So that you could prepare yourselves while there was still time. To live? I don't attach any importance to my life any more. I'm alone. No, I wanted to come back, and to warn you. And see how it is, no one will listen to me. . . ."[2]

The signs of German expansion increased, but no one acknowledged the reality of it for themselves. Bright-sounding rationalizations abounded: "The Germans won't get as far as this. They'll stay in Budapest. There are strategic and political reasons. . . ."[3] Before long, German armed vehicles appeared in the streets. The sight of soldiers wearing steel helmets with their emblem of a death's head caused great anguish, but it was not long before the optimism revived.

> The Germans were already in the town, the Fascists were already in power, the verdict had already been pronounced, yet the Jews of Sighet continued to smile.[4]

There is a realistic optimism that springs from a firsthand knowledge of the merciful workings of a loving God, even, and *especially*, through great trials. The optimists of Sighet, however, derived their *Weltanschauung* from a refusal to acknowledge the fiery dangers, both physical and spiritual, all about them. Tradition, cabbala, and all the positive thinking in the world cannot take the place of He Who alone can reconcile the estranged ones to their Creator.

Each Jew was marked with a yellow star and herded into ghettos. Then, one night, a horrible word was spoken: deportation. Each person was to assemble in the streets in the morning with just a bag of personal belongings. Everything else was to be abandoned. All kinds of heirlooms, menorahs, and jewelry were quickly buried in any plot of earth that could be found, and many old treasured possessions were just left in the street. They had suddenly become valueless.

Under the truncheon blows of the Hungarian police, that tortured company was moved to a smaller ghetto. Skimming the surface of profound grief and fear, the optimistic pronouncements continued. Wiesel observed:

> These optimistic speeches, which no one believed, helped to pass the time. The few days we lived here went by pleasantly enough, in peace. People were better disposed toward one another. There were no longer any questions of wealth, of social distinction, and importance, only people all condemned to the same fate—still unknown.[5]

On the Sabbath, that weary throng marched to the train station. Children clutched at the tired legs of their parents. A convoy of cattle cars was waiting for them there, and, like cattle, eighty of them were crammed into each car. Behind those locked doors, there was almost no air, water, or food, and the heat was unbearable. Body was jammed against body, and it was so crowded that one could not even fall to the floor. That train lurched through the countryside, and, for three days and nights, those people gasped for air in blackness.

> Free from all social constraint, the young people gave way openly to instinct, taking advantage of the darkness to copulate in our midst, without caring about anyone else, as though they were alone in the world. The rest pretended not to notice anything.[6]

This picture of a specific historic event is spiritually as accurate a description of the current state of the human race as I have ever seen. There is a whole world that is locked in dark cattle cars, fornicating away like fools, hurtling on tracks to their doom, and utterly blinded to the fact that they are going to perish by their own refusal to see.

There was a fifty-year-old woman named Madame Schacter in that cattle car. Sporadically, she would point toward the one small barred window and break through the droning monotony of the train wheels with a maddening shriek: "Fire! I can see a fire! I can see a fire!" No one could stand to hear that word. They would gag her and beat her into silence, and, each time, she would revive, and scream, "Look at the fire! Flames, flames everywhere!" Men would look through that little window and see only blackness. That tortured woman would sink into what appeared to be a coma, and everyone else would try to sleep, when, suddenly, again, "The fire! The furnace! Look, over there!" Again they would look and see only the darkness of night.

As that train pulled into Auschwitz, Madame Schacter sat silently in a corner. All of the others had written her off as hopelessly mad. Suddenly, those who had been peering out of the window screamed in terror, "Jews, look! Look through the window! Flames! Look!" Flames gushed out of a tall chimney, and the black night sky was thick with the smell of burning flesh.

My heart went out to Wiesel after the reading of that powerful book. To this day, its vivid images haunt me, and I have shared them with numerous gatherings of people. In the winter of 1975, I attended a presentation that the author gave at a synagogue in New Jersey; it was an event that I had eagerly anticipated for several months.

I was enormously impressed. He was charming, eloquent, simple, and literate; in short, he was the finest expression of all that Jewish life and culture can *humanistically* produce in a man. Sitting at a table on the platform, he gave no formally planned discourse of his own, but answered questions throughout the evening with an adroitness and charm that were a feast for both mind and spirit.

In the course of his remarks, he mentioned his love of the Scriptures, which he reads daily. He added that he is also, several times a week, the student of an orthodox rabbi in the study of the Talmud. The Lord did not give me the liberty to raise a question to him publicly, but, at the conclusion of the meeting, I went to the foot of the platform and asked, "To what degree has your study of the Scriptures given you insight into the cause of the holocaust with which you are identified as the leading Jewish literary figure? I am thinking particularly about the judgment of which God speaks in the concluding chapters in Leviticus and

Deuteronomy." He briefly answered, "I will not or cannot consider *that.*"

With his reply, in a flash, I saw in him the revelation of the utter failure of humanism in its finest expression to cope with the ultimate tragedy of our age (and, therefore, with all tragedy, in the totality of human life as well as in our Jewish predicament). The author's treatment of the holocaust, because it is so superbly literary, is made therefore all the more maudlin and grotesque. Wiesel showed no more real concern to ferret out the true and full meaning of that slaughter than any of the others who had come before him. I saw the tragedy of my people embodied in that man; his openness and honesty as a reporter stopped short of receiving the full revelation of the justice and mercy of God. In the light of the fact of refusing to consider *all* that God offers us, our greatest literature is transformed into an exploitation of suffering and "all our righteousnesses are as filthy rags" (Isaiah 64:6a).

Like Wiesel himself, Moche the beadle and Madame Schacter were messengers who had been given horrifying revelations of evil, but did not know Christ and His victory over it. Their message was true, but it was unbearably incomplete. There was no realistic basis for hope. In a very real sense, their grief-stricken prophecies of doom were inversions of much of modern evangelism. We have preached a cheap salvation that is packed with wonderful rewards, but we have been less than fully truthful in our omission of the reality of a hell of unquenchable fire, eternal burning.

We have been warned by such a man as Finney that if we lose a true understanding of hell, of God's judgment, then the church shall be hopelessly feeble in its witness and not able to touch the world. If the people of God treat these realities as mere "doctrine" and themselves have no awesome sense of the conflagration which is going to come upon the earth and of the everlasting burning and anguish of soul that men who have spurned God's Christ will suffer, we shall collectively become an effete, bloodless, lackluster church—a blot on the face of the earth. The preaching of anything less than the full counsel of God can never give life.

It is not a polite thing to speak about God's soon-coming judgment. How terribly offensive and unsophisticated. As a self-assured atheist, I used to laugh smugly at the caricatures in magazines of men with long beards carrying signs upon which were scrawled, "Repent! For the day of the Lord is at hand!" After conversion, everything was turned around. Things that I had formerly laughed at with disdain I now take terribly to heart, and those issues that I thought were so profound and weighty now seem as old wive's tales.

I am sick to the teeth of all of our talk about "accepting" Jesus. "Hey, why don't you *accept* Jesus? Why don't you be nice and do Him that small favor already? The benefits are great. You'll have a buddy. He'll find a girl friend for you and help you in business. Why don't you accept Him already? He's been waiting so long with His hat in His hand." Because we have left the fire out of our message, we have cheapened the grace we so easily talk about. Men's lives are not changed. Many are "saved," but few are converted from their self-serving existences.

> And Elijah said unto them, Take the prophets of Baal; let not one of them escape. And they took them: and Elijah brought them down to the brook Kishon, and slew them there.
>
> 1 Kings 18:40

The unseen fire that worked purification in the heart of

Elijah enabled him to call fire down from heaven. There could no longer be any doubt about the connection between those consuming flames and the Almighty God. The hearts of the people had indeed been turned back to the Lord. The prophets of Baal, however, had not fallen before the glory of God, but remained standing in rigid defiance. The heavenly fire that worked a salvation of grace in the hearts of the repentant Israelites was, at the same time, the ultimate touchstone of judgment upon those confirmed in their wickedness.

When men like Finney went on their heavenly tasks, whole cities were saved and turned around. People clutched the pillars of the church for fear that they would plummet through the floor and into the pit of Hell, and felt the flames licking at their feet when *the total counsel of God was preached in the power of the Spirit.* In the light of that eternal burning, the staggering necessity of God's merciful forgiveness became starkly evident. The timeless question blazed in men's hearts: "How shall we escape, if we neglect so great salvation?" (Hebrews 2:3a)

People squirmed and fell out of their seats, and Finney was not quick to pick them up, comfort them, and send them away with kind words. He allowed them to writhe there, and they were carried out of meetings in that condition. They remained that way for days until they broke through to God and tasted of the *goodness that leads to repentance.* Those people understood the infinite grace of His salvation, received the riches of His perfect love, and were converted to the unspeakable holiness of His way.

How different a picture that is from our usual situation in modern Christendom. Some evangelical hot shot flies in from out of town, is picked up at the airport, and rushed to the motel. He has just enough time to wash his face, is rushed to the church, and brought up to the platform. He pumps the hand of the minister, is given a five-minute introduction, does his thing, gets paid, goes home—and we hope that some people may have "accepted" Jesus.

We are called, no less than Elijah, to be submitted to the Spirit of the Lord in every way, that hearts may be turned back to God's holy way. Like him, we cannot leave fire out of our message, for to compromise God's whole truth is to counterfeit love. It is not love that avoids warning a perishing world about all that God has clearly affirmed in His word. The half-truths of Moche the beadle and Madame Schacter had not the power to convert a soul, and neither do the sugar-coated sales pitches of modern religion. Nothing less than the whole truth will be enough:

> For, behold, the day cometh, that shall burn as an oven; and all the proud, yea, and all that do wickedly, shall be stubble: and the day that cometh shall burn them up, saith the Lord of hosts, that it shall leave them neither root nor branch.
>
> But unto you that fear my name shall the Sun of righteousness arise with healing in his wings; and ye shall go forth, and grow up as calves of the stall.
>
> And ye shall tread down the wicked; for they shall be ashes under the soles of your feet in the day that I shall do this, saith the Lord of hosts.
>
> Remember ye the law of Moses my servant, which I commanded unto him in Horeb for all Israel, with the statutes and judgments.
>
> Behold, I will send you Elijah the prophet before the coming of the great and dreadful day of the Lord:
>
> And he shall turn the heart of the fathers to the children, and the heart of the children to their

fathers, lest I come and smite the earth with a
curse.

Malachi 4:1-6

At the Door

My Jewish people have a Pesach Seder (Passover dinner
service) each year. In the orthodox homes, there is a feature
which is an indispensable part of the ceremony. A table
setting is reserved for one man, a guest who has never
arrived at these dinners throughout the centuries. It is
called "Elijah's seat," a special place for the forerunner of
the Messiah. At the very end, everyone rises and holds up
what is called "Elijah's cup," the last ceremonial glass of
wine to be imbibed at the Seder. The youngest son goes and
opens the front door, and every person stands, glass in hand,
holding their breath, expectantly waiting for Elijah to
appear. Each year, the same disappointment is repeated:
there is no one at the door.

The Jews have been waiting so long and so eagerly for
Elijah because they know that when that prophet comes the
Messiah shall not be long in following. It shall take more,
however, than the performing of traditional rituals for
salvation to come to my kinsmen. Doors not made of wood
need to be opened, doors of the heart, that the ministry of
Elijah may penetrate to the only place where preparation for
the *Masheach* is meaningful.

It is my prayer that, when Jewish families fling open those
inward doors, they shall be greeted by Elijah-like ministers.
Filled with and moved by the *Ruach Hakodesh*, that
consecrated and unified people, comprised of Jewish and
Gentile believers, a corporate band, shall proclaim the
life-and-death words of repentance and the good news of
God's kingdom.

We who would be used to prepare this wilderness for the

101

return of the Lord must first be willing to be disciplined ourselves in the school of the Spirit. In that school, in obscurity, through grindings, breakings, and shapings at the hand of our loving God, we shall be brought to a true maturity in Him. Like Elijah and like John the Baptist, the mature Body of Christ shall speak with a voice of authority and integrity a message that shall deal death to man's pride and offer eternal life to those who hunger and thirst after God's righteousness:

> The voice of him that crieth in the wilderness, Prepare ye the way of the Lord, make straight in the desert a highway for our God.
>
> Every valley shall be exalted, and every mountain and hill shall be made low: and the crooked shall be made straight, and the rough places plain:
>
> And the glory of the Lord shall be revealed, and all flesh shall see it together: for the mouth of the Lord hath spoken it.
>
> Isaiah 40:3-5

Zion

> . . . The effectual fervent prayer of a righteous man availeth much.
>
> *Elias* [*Elijah*] *was a man subject to like passions as we are*, and he prayed earnestly that it might not rain: and it rained not on the earth by the space of three years and six months.
>
> And he prayed again, and the heaven gave rain, and the earth brought forth her fruit.
>
> James 5:16b-18
> (our italics)

102

After Elijah's great triumph in his confrontation with the prophets of Baal, we read:

> And Elijah said unto Ahab, Get thee up, eat and drink; for there is a sound of abundance of rain.
> So Ahab went up to eat and to drink. And Elijah went up to the top of Carmel; and *he cast himself down upon the earth, and put his face between his knees.* . . .
>
> 1 Kings 18:41, 42
> (our italics)

We do not see God's man in an attitude of rejoicing and of exuberant celebration, but in a posture more associated with dejection; how easily I can picture him there, bent over, and feel what he felt in my own gut. I don't know how many times painful depression has followed upon the heels of a mighty victory of God in and through my own life.

That prophet was a man who knew that he was a pitifully helpless creature unless God gave answer to his prayers. The same Lord Who had sent repentance-bringing fire was now being entreated to send the rain which would heal that land. About a century before Elijah knelt upon that mountain, another Jewish man, Solomon, while still walking in the way of righteousness, prayed fervently for Israel:

> When the heaven is shut up, and there is no rain, because they have sinned against thee; yet if they pray toward this place, and confess thy name, and turn from their sin, when thou dost afflict them;
> Then hear thou from heaven, and forgive the sin of thy servants, and of thy people Israel, when thou hast taught them the good way, wherein they should walk; and send rain upon thy land, which

103

thou hast given unto thy people for an inheritance.
2 Chronicles 6:26, 27

Our Lord hears and answers such prayers spoken in spirit and in truth (see 2 Chronicles 7:12-14). Like all those who move in His Spirit, Elijah and Solomon were in full agreement in their prayers and were united in His purpose, despite the apparent barriers of time and space. The conditions for the rainfall had been eternally established in Heaven, and had been met by the true contrition of that nation. We see, at the conclusion of this eighteenth chapter, the expectancy in the heart of the prophet as he awaited the fulfillment of God's promise, and finally, the bursting forth of the superabounding answer of the Lord:

> And [Elijah] said to his servant, Go up now, look toward the sea. And he went up, and looked, and said, There is nothing. And he said, Go again seven times.
>
> And it came to pass at the seventh time, that he said, Behold, there ariseth a little cloud out of the sea, like a man's hand. And he said, Go up, say unto Ahab, Prepare thy chariot, and get thee down, that the rain stop thee not.
>
> And it came to pass in the mean while, that the heaven was black with clouds and wind, and there was a great rain. And Ahab rode, and went to Jezreel.
>
> And the hand of the Lord was on Elijah; and he girded up his loins, and ran before Ahab to the entrance of Jezreel.
>
> 1 Kings 18:43-46

I praise God for the honesty and completeness of His

Word; lest we suspect that there was something naturally inherent in a man like Elijah that made possible the working of such wonders for God, we are shown in the events at the beginning of 1 Kings 19 that, truly, he was "a man subject to like passions as we are." Ahab had told Jezebel all that God's prophet had accomplished, and the queen, in her wrath, sent a messenger to Elijah with threats of murder. The intimidations of that one woman caused our great hero of the faith to flee with his servant from Jezreel to Beersheba, outside of Jezebel's jurisdiction. He left his servant behind in that city:

> But he himself went a day's journey into the wilderness, and came and sat down under a juniper tree: and he requested for himself that he might die; and said, It is enough; now, O Lord, take away my life; for I am not better than my fathers.
>
> 1 Kings 19:4

Can this be the same man who had just called fire and rain down from Heaven? Absolutely! Every man of God is subject to the same immutable pattern of pits and peaks: somehow, after our most spectacular successes, we are invariably brought down so low that we cannot avoid seeing the fact that all glory and honor belong to God. The Lord, in His love for us, must ever drive home the central point: victories are not won by any intrinsic might or power in a Joseph, an Elijah, or a Katz, but only by His Spirit. We are poor, weak creatures, unless He sustain us.

In the radical spiritual confrontations of these end times, the basic inadequacy of unaided humanity shall be revealed. We shall be stripped down to a total dependency upon our God. Each of us, when pressed hard enough by the evil of this world, shall come out looking no more noble than poor Elijah. The weakness that his crisis revealed in him is our own. Somewhere in the depths of every soul is a juniper tree, beneath which, when the going gets too rough, we shall lie down, and plead for death. Flesh is flesh.

> And as he lay and slept under a juniper tree, behold, then an angel touched him, and said unto him, Arise and eat.
>
> And he looked, and, behold, there was a cake baken on the coals, and a cruse of water at his head. And he did eat and drink, and laid him down again.
>
> And the angel of the Lord came again the second time, and touched him, and said, *Arise and eat; because the journey is too great for thee.*
>
> *And he arose, and did eat and drink, and went in the strength of that meat* [food] *forty days and forty nights unto Horeb the mount of God.*
>
> 1 Kings 19:5-8
(our italics)

God is calling us to a last forty-day journey. Forty is always a number of testing and trial in the Scriptures, and, truly, we shall not be able to make it on our own strength, wisdom, or abilities.

The mountain that we are seeking is not Horeb, but Zion:

> But ye are come unto mount Sion, and unto the city of the living God, the heavenly Jerusalem, and to an innumerable company of angels,
>
> To the general assembly and church of the firstborn, which are written in heaven, and to God the Judge of all, and to the spirits of just men made perfect,

And to Jesus the mediator of the new covenant, and to the blood of sprinkling, that speaketh better things than that of Abel.

Hebrews 12:22-24

We are traveling toward the full revelation of what has already happened in the Spirit to every born-again man, woman, and child: God "hath raised us up together, and made us sit *together in heavenly places in Christ Jesus*" (Ephesians 2:6). It is a divine paradox that, *in Him*, we have already arrived at that timeless city that our feet of flesh are only slowly approaching, step by step, in time.

When we shall come to that final mount at the end of our arduous journey in the taking of the land, God shall assemble His house on that holy hill. It shall not be one built with stones that have been cut by hand, but with *living* stones, Jewish and Gentile. The glory of that temple shall be greater than all the splendor of those former buildings. God's Shechinah fire shall inhabit the Holy of Holies, and He shall send that light forth to cover a dark earth.

In this final pilgrimage, many shall be dejected and cry out, "Take me, I'm ready to die!" Our God shall continually remind us, however, that, although the journey is indeed too great for us, we shall be sustained if we eat and drink of the heavenly provision.

Have you been eating and drinking of the Lord? Most of us have given Him a lot of nice pecks on the cheek, and have enjoyed the latest "Christian" entertainment, but, I warn you, none of that shall be enough to bring us through the hard demands of our wilderness trek. We are going to have to come to such a relationship with Him, and come to such a place *in* Him, that we can say with Paul, "For to me to live is Christ." Unless He is the life of my life, strength of my strength, wisdom of my wisdom, and speaking of my speaking, I shall be blown away by the first Ahab or Jezebel who stands in my path.

We are being called to a deep communion with our Lord, a life which shall share in the fellowship of His sufferings as well as the glory of His resurrection. The world shall not believe our words about the Messiah unless as members of one Body, we move in the unity of His Spirit. Jesus prayed to the Father for the bringing forth of a corporate man, fully partaking of the life of God:

> That they all may be one; as thou, Father, art in me, and I in thee, that they also may be one in us: that the world may believe that thou hast sent me.
>
> And the glory which thou gavest me I have given them; that they may be one, even as we are one:
>
> I in them, and thou in me, that they may be made perfect in one; and that the world may know that thou hast sent me, and hast loved them, as thou hast loved me.
>
> John 17:21-23

At the Lord's table, we shall receive sustenance for, not only the "forty-day" journey, but for eternity:

> And Jesus said unto them, I am the bread of life: he that cometh to me shall never hunger; and he that believeth on me shall never thirst.
>
> I am the living bread which came down from heaven: if any man eat of this bread, he shall live for ever: and *the bread that I will give is my flesh, which I will give for the life of the world.*
>
> John 6:35, 51
> (our italics)

108

Lest we ever forget the path that our Lord trod on this earth, we must continue to go back to that table which was set for us on Golgotha. We shall faint, stumble, and fall away from God and each other, unless we are wholly in communion with the One Who laid down His life for us. So much more is involved here than merely going through the motions of what has become, for many people, nothing more than a well-learned and smoothly executed religious ritual. Every child of God's Kingdom is called to a total and intimate spiritual intercourse with the living Messiah. This is the key: *Christ in us and we in Him.* In the giving to Him of *all* that we are, and in the receiving into our innermost recesses of *all* that He is, we shall walk together in the power of His love, inviting a world which is languishing between two opinions to God's feast of eternal life.

Then Jesus said unto them, Verily, verily, I say unto you, Except ye eat the flesh of the Son of man, and drink his blood, ye have no life in you.

Whoso eateth my flesh, and drinketh my blood, hath eternal life; and I will raise him up at the last day.

For my flesh is meat indeed, and my blood is drink indeed.

He that eateth my flesh, and drinketh my blood, dwelleth in me, and I in him.

As the living Father hath sent me, and I live by the Father: so he that eateth me, even he shall live by me.

This is that bread which came down from heaven: not as your fathers did eat manna, and are dead: he that eateth of this bread shall live for ever.

John 6:53-58
(our italics)

109

In the strength of *that* food, though we walk through the valley of the shadow of death, we shall make it to the mount.

Therefore the redeemed of the Lord shall return, and come with singing unto Zion; and everlasting joy shall be upon their head: they shall obtain gladness and joy; and sorrow and mourning shall flee away.

Isaiah 51:11

Chapter Three

And the Prisoners Heard Them: Paul and Silas and the End Times

Led by the Spirit

At Lystra, two Jewish men, Paul and Silas, took into their company the son of a Jewish mother and Greek father, Timothy (Acts 16:1-3). A small band of disciples was forming which would join Paul on his second missionary journey.

> And as they went through the cities, they delivered them the decrees for to keep, that were ordained of the apostles and elders which were at Jerusalem.
> *And so were the churches established in the faith, and increased in number daily.*
>
> Acts 16:4,5
> (our italics)

These men were doing the work of God in Asia Minor and were meeting with conspicuous success. The next four verses contain three significant manifestations of the Holy Spirit.

> Now when they had gone throughout Phrygia and the region of Galatia, and *were forbidden of the Holy Ghost to preach the word in Asia* [a province within Asia Minor],
> After they were come to Mysia, *they assayed to go into Bithynia: but the Spirit suffered them not.*
> And they passing by Mysia came down to Troas.
> And a vision appeared to Paul in the night; There stood a man of Macedonia, and prayed him, saying, *Come over into Macedonia, and help us.*
>
> Acts 16:6-9
> (our italics)

Twice the Spirit checked the steps of these travelers, and

then He directed them to the place of His choosing. "Forbidden of the Holy Ghost to preach the word in Asia! This can't be. The Bible plainly says that we should go into all the world and preach the gospel to every creature, *so I'm going!* I'll determine where I'll go and how I'll get there. God himself has given me a blank check." This, almost needless to say, is a dangerous attitude.

God has indeed given us a general invitation, but the specific fulfilling of it *must* be directed by the Holy Spirit each step of the way. So many of us are much more responsive to the Spirit when He bids us go than when He calls us to a halt. We want to go, go, go. We want to do great exploits for the Lord, preferably before the eye of the admiring masses. To be dead and hid with Christ in God is not quite as easy to receive, especially when you have been successful in establishing the churches in Asia Minor. If the Holy Spirit can shut your mouth in the very place of your greatest preaching achievements, I would say that He has possession of His vessel.

What kind of spirit would lead a band of God's men away from the continent of their proven success and point them toward a place where neither their names nor the name of their Lord had ever been heard? Many might say, "That's not the Spirit of God. That's the spirit of Satan trying to distract God's servant, take him away from the field of his greatest use, and send him to some remote place where he's going to be lost in obscurity. Macedonia? Never!"

Once again, one of the key questions of these end times is raised: how can we determine whether we are being spoken to by the Spirit of God or by the spirit of the evil one? We know that Satan is a vicious counterfeiter, and that his artful attempts to imitate the voice of God have often fooled the Lord's children. How could Paul and the others *know* that it

113

was the Holy Spirit keeping them from preaching in the provinces of Asia and Bithynia, and directing them to Macedonia? They knew in the only way that men can: like Elijah before them, they were so familiar with the accents of the still small voice of God that they had no doubt Who was speaking to them.

A man who has that kind of intimacy with the Lord's voice is one who has been long processed at His hand, one who has known breakings, grindings, and cuttings away of the flesh. It is only by going through these wilderness testings that a true and consistent sensitivity to the things of the Spirit emerges.

Correctly discerning the voice of God is literally a matter of life and death. If Paul had missed the Spirit's signal that came to him at the edge of the Asian continent, in Troas, countless numbers of God's children would still be in darkness. Because he heard it and obeyed, the Gospel went from Asia to Europe for the first time. Men who had previously drunk their beer out of skulls were saved out of paganism and death and turned to the living God. As a result of that act of obedience, the Word of life began its course not only through the European continent, but throughout the Western world.

Knit Together

And after he had seen the vision, immediately we endeavoured to go into Macedonia, assuredly gathering that the Lord had called us for to preach the gospel unto them.

Acts 16:10

That vision came only to one man, Paul, but each of the others, without hesitation, set their faces towards

Macedonia. "And after *he* had seen the vision, *we* endeavoured to go. . . ." What a vivid picture of the order of God in the Body of Christ.

Those men were knit together, joint by joint. Their relationships were so intimate, tested, and true, that those disciples knew in the depths of their hearts that the ascended Christ Himself had invested Paul, their "servant," with true apostolic authority (Ephesians 4:10,11). When Paul had a vision, no one suggested that it was indigestion: ". . . *we* endeavoured to go into Macedonia, assuredly gathering that the Lord had called *us*. . . ."

Paul taught, "Be ye followers of me, even as I also am of Christ" (1 Corinthians 11:1). He knew that he was directing this counsel to men and women who were indwelt by the Spirit of God, and who could exercise the spiritual discernment which is a gift of God to every believer. He repeatedly warned the Lord's disciples against evil and deceitful workers, but was so sure of his own submission to God, that he could boldly tell them to follow him *as he followed Christ.* If you find yourself in a position of leadership amidst God's people, it behooves you to ask: "Am I, in spirit and in truth, following the living God, or am I simply following the established programs and traditions of men?" The fundamental nature of your relationship to the flock of God is no light matter. The word of the Lord came to Ezekiel:

> Son of man, prophesy against the shepherds of Israel, prophesy, and say unto them, Thus saith the Lord God unto the shepherds; Woe be to the shepherds of Israel that do feed themselves! should not the shepherds feed the flocks?
>
> Therefore, O ye shepherds, hear the word of the Lord;

> Thus saith the Lord God; Behold, I am against
> the shepherds; and I will require my flock at their
> hand, and cause them to cease from feeding the
> flock; neither shall the shepherds feed themselves
> any more; for I will deliver my flock from their
> mouth, that they may not be meat for them.
>
> Ezekiel 34:2,9,10

Paul's model for true spiritual authority was the One who washed His disciples' feet. He was committed to following the example of the great Servant:

> For we preach not ourselves, but Christ Jesus
> the Lord; and ourselves your servants for Jesus'
> sake.
>
> 2 Corinthians 4:5

He could ask men to obediently follow him, for his own heart was yielded to Jesus, the perfectly obedient Son:

> Let this mind be in you, which was also in Christ
> Jesus:
> Who, being in the form of God, thought it not
> robbery to be equal with God:
> But made himself of no reputation, and took
> upon him the form of a servant, and was made in
> the likeness of men:
> And being found in fashion as a man, he
> humbled himself, and became obedient unto
> death, even the death of the cross.
>
> Philippians 2:5-8

Filled with and knit together by the Spirit of God, those men moved in unity to Macedonia, though only Paul had seen the vision.

One night, after I had preached this message, a very distraught middle-aged woman came over to me. She related that her husband believed he had received a vision. He maintained that they should leave their business, their beautiful home, their swimming pool, and their modest lay Christian ministry, where they had baptized believers, had Bible studies, and conducted prayer meetings. They were to leave all, sell all, and go to Youth With A Mission in Europe to study evangelism. That woman thought her husband had flipped out. She said, "When *I* see the vision, *then* we'll go!"

I said, "Dear sister, with that attitude you'll never see the vision." She thought that I was attacking her spirituality, but I was simply showing her something about the order of God. When the heavenly vision is given to the head of a family, all of the members which are knit joint by joint to that head will move with it, not as a mechanical and lifeless political act, but as an act of love born of and witnessed by the Holy Spirit.

This brings us to another crucial question for the Body of Christ in the end times: when an explicit word or vision will come from the Lord, calling us to fateful tasks in which life-and-death issues are being propounded, will we be found to be in the proper order of God? Are we so submitted to the elders whom God has placed in our midst that when *they* receive the vision, *we* shall assuredly gather that the Lord has called *us*?

Of course, before we can submit to a leader, we must first be submitted unto God Himself; it is He who shall reveal His true apostles, prophets, evangelists, pastors, and teachers to each of us by the Spirit. Paul was scrupulously careful not to usurp the headship of Christ in the lives of those whom the Lord had entrusted into his care:

117

Now I praise you, brethren, that ye remember me in all things, and keep the ordinances, as I delivered them to you.

But I would have you know, that the head of every man is Christ; and the head of the woman is the man; and the head of Christ is God.

1 Corinthians 11:2, 3

I know that our elders are lacking, but, *if they are the ones whom God has established*, it behooves us to be submitted to them in much the same way that it behooves a wife to be submitted to her husband, even though he may not be as "spiritual" as she would like. Those who enjoy criticizing their elders need to see that God will not minister the fulness of maturity, depth, and spirituality necessary to leaders until we are all submitted one to another in love. Truly, the Head of every man is Christ, and He is faithful to teach, to guide, and to correct:

Obey them that have the rule over you, and submit yourselves: for they watch for your souls, *as they that must give account*, that they may do it with joy, and not with grief: for that is unprofitable for you.

Hebrews 13:17
(our italics)

There is probably no hotter word in Christendom today than "submission." As is true of every godly principle, it is open to damaging perversion by selfish men. Martin Luther would have wound up in spiritual bondage had he valued the authority of the Pope above the Spirit and the Word of God. God calls us to neither anarchistic rebellion nor to blind and

118

slavish obedience to men, but to a walk in the Spirit, knit together by the living Christ.

The Chief City

> Therefore loosing from Troas, we came with a straight course to Samothracia, and the next day to Neapolis;
>
> And from thence to Philippi, which is the chief city of that part of Macedonia, and a colony: and we were in that city abiding certain days.
>
> Acts 16:11,12

The eye of God is roving to and fro over the face of the earth and over His Christian people, looking for the Pauls and Silases of this generation who, when they receive the Word of the Lord, immediately set forth on a straight course. Again, I recall the response of Elijah: he was directed by God to go to Zarephath: "So he arose and went . . ." (1 Kings 17:10a). It is no accident that the fulness and power of the Spirit marked the lives of each of these men: this shall always be the case with those who obey God unconditionally.

What is the nature of our generation? "When my kids grow up, when I have a sufficient bundle in the bank account, when I've established my security, when I receive my pension, when I retire, *then* I'll devote myself." Christianity has been fettered by its own indecision, compromise, and deceit; God is looking for hearts that long to respond to His call with no ifs, ands, or buts.

The Lord does not generally follow His simple commands with lengthy and complicated explanations. He knows the end from the beginning though we do not. Recently, while attending a gospel conference in New York City, the Holy Spirit directed me to take several significant Christian

119

people on a tour of that city's Jewish life. I did not know where to begin in that home of two-and-a-half million Jews, but the Lord said, "Now."

I nosed the car out of the driveway of the hotel. I had no clear direction of where to go, but I knew that we had to be in motion. As we departed from that building, I was glad to find that we were on a one-way street. Before I had traveled a few blocks, I found that I was being directed toward the East Side of New York, where we stopped to visit a Jewish publishing house, walked some of the streets of that ancient Jewish ghetto, and ate at a kosher delicatessen whose food was enjoyed by all.

Before that day was out, we ended up in my mother's apartment in Brooklyn, where those men had a first-hand experience of a typical Jewish woman's reaction to the gospel challenge. It was altogether an exceptionally rich day and could not have been more perfectly appointed of the Lord. It began by nosing a car out of a driveway.

That incident is, of course, hardly on the scale of introducing the gospel to the European continent, but how illustrative it is of how He honors even the smallest acts of faithfulness. God directed those disciples to Philippi, the chief city of that part of Macedonia. Wherever God may call you by the Holy Spirit, be it however humble—to the washing of dishes, to the changing of diapers, to the sweeping of floors, to a word of apology, to asking forgiveness, to something gracious, or to something humiliating—*for you, that is the chief city.*

If you will not obey that call, you need not think that you will hear another. Many of us have been stalemated; God has been silent to us because there was a time in His speaking that we chose not to hear and not to obey. We would have loved a grandiose call to action, but God may have called us to humiliation, and we chose to think of that bidding as indigestion. If we had opened our ears and hearts, we would have known that that was the "chief city" at that time. It behooves us to seek the face of the Lord and ask Him to repeat anything that He may have previously spoken that we have chosen to ignore, that we might do that first thing, and hear again His clear call.

Joined to the Lord

> And on the sabbath we went out of the city by a river side, where prayer was wont to be made; and we sat down, and spake unto the women which resorted thither.
>
> Acts 16:13

"Oh, Paul. I thought that you were a man of God. I thought that you understood something about the principles of God. God brings you all the way from Asia to Europe, you come to the chief city, which is swarming with all kinds of people and activities, and you go *out* of the city? Man, you don't know the ABCs of evangelism. You'd better enroll in a course on how to spread the Word."

We have been much intoxicated by numbers. The spirit of the modern world has permeated God's people. I know that my God will send His men halfway around the world for one soul. The question is not "one, one thousand, or one million;" the question is, "are we so obedient to the heavenly vision that we are in the place where God wants us?" The numbers are irrelevant.

Strictly speaking, we cannot say that it was a "vision" that impelled Paul to go to that riverside; the Scriptures do not indicate that. Nor do we read, "The Holy Spirit said to Paul, 'Get thee out of the city and go to the riverside.' " We have already seen in this sixteenth chapter the working of the Spirit that checks and forbids, and the working which says,

121

"Come." Here we see an operation of the Spirit that may be neither vision nor speaking.

How did Paul know to go out of the city when he should have remained there by every naturally wise evangelical reckoning? It may be that he simply had a hunch. How unspiritual that sounds; but, for the man who is possessed by the Holy Spirit, a "hunch" or an "impulse" can be everything. Truly, ". . . he that is joined unto the Lord is one spirit" (1 Corinthians 6:17).

My life with God began in Jerusalem, where I heard His still small voice call me by name. I have heard that same voice on several occasions in the course of my walk and ministry explicitly saying do this, go there, speak that. It is a great delight to have God so explicitly speak to you; it is not quite as pleasant when you have come to a place of commitment and have not heard a single word of direction from the Lord.

You might be sitting on a platform, waiting to be called to the pulpit, hearing yourself being introduced: "We have this man of God with us today, and we know that we are going to hear from God through him. We know that God has given him a word. . . ." All this time you are thinking to yourself, "Yeah, I wish I knew what it is." The moments tick away, you are finally called up, and you still have not heard from God. What do you do in a moment like that? *If you know that you are joined to the Lord*, you have no alternative but to speak whatever is in your mind and heart.

If your life truly belongs to God, then it is foolishness to speak in terms of *you here* doing things for *God there*.

What? know ye not that your body is the temple
of the Holy Ghost which is in you, which ye have of
God, and ye are not your own?

1 Corinthians 6:19

> For in him we live, and move, and have our
> being. . . .
>
> Acts 17:28a

> . . . Christ in you, the hope of glory.
>
> Colossians 1:27b

"For me to live is Christ . . ." (Philippians 1:21a). For me to speak is Christ. For me to carry on a conversation is Christ. For me even to be sociable is Christ. I was once a very engaging personality. An hour with Art Katz over a cup of coffee would be filled with bright and witty conversation on almost any topic. Now Katz is lousy company; I am gray, lifeless, inert, *except that He is my life.*

If there is any graciousness in me, it is His graciousness. If there is any real wisdom, it is His wisdom. When it pleases Him not to be engaging, speaking bright things, then neither am I:

> For ye are dead, and your life is hid with Christ
> in God.
> When Christ, who is our life, shall appear, then
> shall ye also appear with him in glory.
>
> Colossians 3:3,4

We have no glory independent of His glory. He *is* my life.

We are not to disparage the significance of "hunches," "accidents," and circumstantial leadings of God. As the people of the Spirit, we are to be entirely animated and led by the Spirit. We are being called to get every fleshly thing out of the way, all of our own clever thoughts and good intentions.

"Oh man, we're in Philippi. Let's see, where is the biggest meeting place located? I think we ought to rent the local ball park, put up big signs and placards, and pass out handbills. Let's get the crowds." This is conventional evangelical wisdom, and it is not necessarily wrong, if God has established it in any given moment. We are summoned to *a walk in the Spirit, moment by moment.*

What God blessed, anointed, and made into a life-giving thing in the past, He may not use today. Early in my ministerial walk, I had to learn that just because the Lord gave me a message yesterday that blessed the people, I cannot, as a matter of course, bring it out today in order to be a blessing.

Any kind of methodology, any kind of technique, anything that is cut and dried and can be put down in a set number of laws or principles is not likely to be the perfect thing of God in a specific situation. There may be a time when the Lord will employ it, but not every time. Jesus said:

> The wind bloweth where it listeth, and thou hearest the sound thereof, but canst not tell whence it cometh, and whither it goeth: *so is every one that is born of the Spirit.*
>
> John 3:8
> (our italics)

Assuredly gathering that the Lord has called us to a particular place and that we have, in truth, presented our bodies as a living sacrifice, we can boldly speak and do what is in our heart at that moment. If you are a mature believer whose life is not your own, and whose only purpose is His glory, then this is wise counsel. If you are fleshly, carnal, and immature, wanting to do your own thing, wanting to be seen and applauded, then for me to suggest to you that you ought to do what is in your heart is the most dangerous counsel I can give. It is only when your will is His will, your thought is

His thought, and your heart is His heart that it is safe to say, "do what is in your heart."

> The steps of a good man are ordered by the Lord: and he delighteth in his way.
>
> Psalm 37:23

At the River: Lydia and the Word of God

> And a certain woman named Lydia, a seller of purple, of the city of Thyatira, which worshipped God, heard us: whose heart the Lord opened, that she attended unto the things which were spoken of Paul.
>
> Acts 16:14

How many times have we truly attended to the things which have been spoken by the teachers whom God has sent us? Has there ever been a generation more indulged, spiritually speaking, than this one? With all the knowledge pouring in from speakers, tapes, and literature, where is the accompanying maturity and growth?

It almost seems as if we should call a moratorium and let there be no more speaking until we have caught up in our experience to what we have already heard. We think that the whole purpose of our Christian existence is to be called together in meetings, that we might hear more "teaching." It was not so from the beginning.

Lydia, whose heart was opened by the Lord, *attended* to the things which were spoken by Paul. I know she attended, because her hearing eventuated in her *acting*: in the very next line we read, "And when she was baptized . . ." (verse 15a). If you say, "Well, big deal, what's baptism?" maybe you need a Jewish guy to remind you of its enormous profundity. It is the ultimate act of separation and commitment.

Unsaved and benighted Jewish people often have, in a real sense, a greater grasp of the meaning of baptism than many of those in the faith; somewhere in the depths of their souls, they know that it is truly a burial unto death. A dear friend of mine was raised in an orthodox Jewish home in Sweden. When he became a believer in Jesus, the news was not well received, but those repercussions were nothing compared to the family's reaction to the news of his baptism. Although he had been a beloved son, his parents conducted the traditional burial service for him.

Ten years later, my friend called his father on the phone; the father asked who it was and my friend said, "This is your son." The older man answered, "My son is dead," and hung up. May that old Jewish man come to a complete knowledge of what happened to his son:

> Know ye not, that so many of us as were baptized into Jesus Christ were baptized into his death?
>
> Therefore we are buried with him by baptism into death: that like as Christ was raised up from the dead by the glory of the Father, even so we also should walk in newness of life.
>
> Romans 6:3, 4

I am so in love with baptism that you might well call me Art the Baptist. If I can't find a pool in which to immerse you, I'll plunge you into your own bathtub, or into mine. Recently, after a meeting in Germany, eight believers went into the bathtub, one after the other. I did not come with any intention of doing such a thing, but they knew, after the Lord had spoken to them, that there was something required from them, an act of radical separation that could only be accomplished by going under the waters of judgment and death, and rising to newness of life in Him.

In the baptism performed in spirit and truth, we are called not to a mindless religious ceremony, but to an unconditional commitment to the living Christ. Lydia knew that Paul and Silas would be leaving town in a couple of days, and that she would remain there with the stigma of public baptism upon her. May God raise up Lydias for our generation, precious children of the Lord who hear His way and do it, despite the cost.

> And when she was baptized, and her household, she besought us, saying, If ye have judged me to be faithful to the Lord, come into my house, and abide there. *And she constrained us.*
>
> Acts 16:15
> (our italics)

Her whole household was baptized with her. I can only assume that they were so kindred with her in spirit that they saw the same Light with her, were obedient to the word of the Lord, and received the same blessing. What a rare and beautiful boldness is evident in that woman of God immediately following the riverside baptism: she *constrained* the disciples to visit and abide in her house.

Luke, the chronicler of these events, who joined this band of men at Troas, used the same word in writing about the meeting of the two disciples with Jesus on the road to Emmaus:

> And they drew nigh unto the village, whither they went: and he [Jesus] made as though he would have gone further.

> *But they constrained him*, saying, Abide with
> us: for it is toward evening, and the day is far
> spent. And he went in to tarry with them.
>
> And it came to pass, as he sat at meat with
> them, he took bread, and blessed it, and brake,
> and gave to them.
>
> And their eyes were opened, and they knew
> him. . . .
>
> Luke 24:28-31a
> (our italics)

We live in a generation that does not know how to constrain
God, to groan to Him out of our gut, or, as we Jews say, out
of the kishkes. Has there ever been a more plastic culture
than ours? Everything is lived from the surface of our lives.
This is the age of convenience and ease: instant breakfast; fly
now, pay later; no stoop, no fuss, no bother. It shall not last.

How do we give an invitation? "Well, if you're in the
neighborhood, why don't you drop in?" (hoping against hope
that they won't come over when the football game is on and
keep us from our pleasure). In Lydia's part of the world,
when someone comes under your roof, enjoys your
hospitality, and breaks bread with you, you are considered
one with them; what they are, you are, and whatever stigma
they receive you receive also. Yet, Lydia constrained them
to abide there.

It is no wonder that God chose her as the first of His fruit
in Philippi.

> For the eyes of the Lord run to and fro
> throughout the whole earth, to shew himself
> strong in the behalf of them whose heart is perfect
> toward him.
>
> 2 Chronicles 16:9a

God sent His choicest servants from Asia to Greece to bring the words which would bring that woman more perfectly into the Way, that she might be the beginning of the Body of Christ there.

The Efficacy of Grief

> And it came to pass, as we went to prayer, a certain damsel possessed with a spirit of divination met us, which brought her masters much gain by soothsaying:
>
> The same followed Paul and us, and cried, saying, These men are the servants of the most high God, which shew unto us the way of salvation.
>
> And this did she many days.
>
> Acts 16:16-18a

This was not just a woman speaking. Paul and the other brethren were hounded for many days by the sound of that filthy spirit speaking through her. The thought of those words of truth being uttered by a demoniacal, cracked, high-pitched voice sends a chill down my spine.

> But *Paul, being grieved*, turned and said to the spirit, I command thee in the name of Jesus Christ to come out of her. And he came out the same hour.
>
> Acts 16:18b
(our italics)

I used to think that this verse meant something like "Paul, being bugged," or "Paul, being irritated." "Paul, being *grieved*" is very different; in that difference lies an important principle of God.

How is it that when we have said, "Come out of her" they have not come out? How is it that when we have prayed "Be healed," they have not been healed? We may have what we call faith, a basic belief, but do we have love? In the absence of love, there can be no godly grief, and it is ". . . faith which *worketh* by love" (Galatians 5:6).

Paul, being grieved; Paul, being stricken; Paul, being cut in his heart; Paul, anguishing over the sight of a woman whose life was not her own, who was a cheap piece of merchandise exploited by vicious men for profit, commanded the evil spirit to come out, and it came out in the same hour. Our Lord Himself is the supreme exemplar of this principle:

> And Jesus went forth, and saw a great multitude, and *was moved with compassion* toward them, and he healed their sick.
>
> Matthew 14:14
> (our italics)

We may be children of faith, but are we also children of love? Are we grieved? You might say, "When I'll hear a woman like that, you can be assured I'll be grieved also." Do not be deceived: they are everywhere about us. You do not have to wait to hear those demoniacal shrieks.

There are people who are wearing pin-striped suits, whose voices are never raised above quiet monotones, who live perfectly ordered, ethical, cultural lives, who are as much slaves to Satan as that woman. Don't you see them? Their lives are not their own; they are marching to a beat that sounds out of the depths of hell, and do not even know it.

That woman *knew* that she was possessed, but the pity is the greater for those who have no knowledge that they are

130

securely in the hands of the evil one. The cruel taskmaster is cracking an invisible whip over the backs of millions of people: the result is a world of fear, insecurity, keeping up with the Joneses, rat races, broken homes, and lives hidden behind shut doors and pulled shades. Mankind is groaning Do you have ears to hear?

When you see that man in the pin-striped suit, and he seems to have everything in order, and is well-spoken, do you assume that all is well? If we are children of the Spirit, we need also to see by the eye of the Spirit that we are surrounded by people whose souls are shrieking and crying with hellish torture, although they give every outward appearance of having everything in its place. They need to be set free in the power of the Spirit by those who have godly authority and faith, and who are grieved in love.

These Men, Being Jews, Do Exceedingly Trouble Our Cities

What is the reward for such outstanding service to God? Will we receive a plaque for meritorious service and be dubbed the Man of the Year by the Junior Chamber of Commerce because we have been obedient to the heavenly vision? Joseph was thrown into a dungeon. Elijah was called before Ahab and was asked, "Art thou he that troubleth Israel?"

> And when her masters saw that the hope of their gains was gone, they caught Paul and Silas, and drew them into the marketplace unto the rulers,
> And brought them to the magistrates, saying, These men, being Jews, do exceedingly trouble our city,

And teach customs which are not lawful for us to receive, neither to observe, being Romans.

And the multitude rose up together against them: and the magistrates rent off their clothes, and commanded to beat them.

And when they had laid many stripes upon them, they cast them into prison, charging the jailor to keep them safely:

Who, having received such a charge, thrust them into the inner prison, and made their feet fast in the stocks.

Acts 16:19-24

If this is a definitive pattern of God, then we should have every reasonable expectation that the obedience to the Holy Spirit rendered by us shall result in the same consequence that it did for Paul and Silas. It was true for Jesus, and it shall be true for every one of His disciples.

Then he [Jesus] said unto them, O fools, and slow of heart to believe all that the prophets have spoken:

Ought not Christ to have suffered these things, and to enter into his glory?

And said unto them, Thus it is written, and thus *it behoved Christ to suffer*, and to rise from the dead the third day.

Luke 24:25, 26, 46
(our italics)

Obedience to the Lord will not result in being cheered and applauded by men in this world's market places. It will result in reproach, persecution, suffering, and perhaps

132

death. Be forewarned that it may not come only from the world; you may receive the same from those who call themselves Christians. "And the *multitude* rose up together against them."

As God is moving to bring together the unity of His body, Satan is also moving to bring about the unity of his. They are going to battle it out at the end of the ages. There is no issue that will more coalesce those forces which are antagonistic to God than the common opposition to God's people. Political, social, economic, and religious powers who have never agreed on anything shall join together against the true believers.

I have often said, "If you have two Jews, you get three arguments." There is hardly a thing that the three branches of Judaism agree about, but there is one issue about which the orthodox, the conservative, and the reform Jews are in full accord: if there is a Jew who believes in Jesus, he is written out of the Jewish community; he is no longer a Jew. "And the multitude rose up together against them."

Herod and Pilate, Jewish and gentile rulers, were natural enemies. Then the day arrived when they were both directly confronted with the presence of Jesus. The pattern is clear:

> And the same day Pilate and Herod were made friends together: for before they were at enmity between themselves.
>
> Luke 23:12

Returning from Jerusalem to California, stunned by the discovery of God, I had my first disappointment as a young believer. I had been fully and naively expecting that, when I took my place in a certain Pentecostal congregation there, I would see the continuation of the Book of Acts.

What I found was sort of a country club sport, an empty

routine that had no impact on the community whatsoever; neither was there, therefore, any persecution nor any reproach.

I believe with all my heart that this age is going to end exactly as it began, in an apostolic manner, in the power of the Spirit. God's people shall be directed, not by human programs, devices, or ambitions, but by the heavenly Father. I am not expecting that the end-time Body of Christ will have a large number of members. As it was at the inception of this age, so it shall be at the end: an island of faith, truth, and Spirit life set in a sea of hostility, bitterness, and opposition. None of our natural resources will be enough to keep us from going under. There is only one factor that will enable us to endure until the end: "Not by might, nor by power, but by my spirit, saith the Lord of hosts" (Zechariah 4:6b).

As part of a series of programs that I did for Christian Broadcasting Network, I delivered this message from Acts 16. The night before that program is almost as memorable to me as the program itself. Exhausted and wiped out from a day of activities at CBN's studio in Portsmouth, Virginia, I could not wait to hit the sack.

I left a trail of clothing from the door of my hotel room to the bed, and, with my last ounce of energy, I hit the light switch and toppled into bed. My head hit the pillow and—nothing happened. I punched the pillow and put my head back. Nothing. Sleep seemed utterly unattainable. I writhed and turned this way and that way without any success at all. In disgust, I put on the light. It was two o'clock. Exasperated, spent, I said to myself, "Well, that's what you get, Katz. Some Jewish boy. It serves you right for going to bed without washing. Didn't your mother teach you better than that?"

So I got out of bed, fully repentant, and took a hot bath (I mean a HOT bath. I almost fainted in the tub). As I climbed out and staggered towards the bed, I expected that, in that final lurch, I would crumble onto the floor, and there, in whatever position I landed, I would remain for the rest of the night, dead out. I made it to the bed, however, hit the light, punched the pillow, and—nothing, not a drop of sleep all night. When I turned the light on again, it was 6:20, and I had to be at the studio at 7:30. Defeated, I turned to the Lord.

I think that my best moments in prayer have come when Satan has worked me over, roasted me on a spit, and buffeted me in the middle of the night hours, and, conceding defeat in my attempts to sleep, I would get down on my knees and call upon God. Our Lord will use even the work of the enemy for our good. Truly, God's strength is made perfect in our weakness.

Before that morning's taping, I said to the technicians, "Have you got a whip and handcuffs in this place?" They gave me a look which said, "Katz, you're too much. Whip and handcuffs? What do you think this is, an armory?"

There happened to be a police station about a block away, and one of them went and borrowed a pair of handcuffs. Then the prop man made a whip out of a broom handle and pieces of leather, attaching pieces of metal and glass to each strip of that vicious-looking cat-o'-nine-tails. There was no man-made script to follow; God was ordering something new.

Feeling the heft of those instruments in my hands, I had the cameraman focus on them at the beginning of the program. Addressing an audience that was to me invisible, I said, "I suppose you're wondering what these implements have to do with a gospel telecast. My answer to you is, 'Everything.' They have ever and always had to do with the promulgation of the gospel. It will not be different at the

135

end of the ages for those who will be obedient to the Holy Spirit."

Many of us will bear in our bodies, as Paul did, the marks of Jesus Christ. These *are* the last hours. In the titanic collision between light and darkness, there will be casualties. Men will not be able to endure such extremity, except they be sustained by the Holy Spirit.

"And when they had laid many stripes upon them. . . ." How prone we are to simply gloss over words like these without so much as wincing. Most of us have been insulated from any real understanding of this kind of experience. I used to be a boxing fan, and every Wednesday and Friday night I would be glued to the television set; it was "fight night." Man, when that guy sagged against the rope, my heart pounded with excitement; when the mouthpiece went flying across the ring, I could hardly wait for the knockout; how I loved the sense of suspense when the loser was tottering and about to go down.

One night, I went to the arena to watch a fight in the flesh for the first time. I have not been a boxing fan since that night. The first blow landed on the ribs with a loud impact; when the glove was pulled away, I saw a big red welt the size of the glove, and I began to get a sickly feeling in my stomach. That was followed by more whacks and cracks and socks. When I saw the mouthpiece go flying, I was almost doubled up with nausea in my seat.

I was sickened by the sight of real blood and spittle, real ooze, real crunching blows. Somehow, that real impact never got through to me while watching the TV set. Here is the point: this generation has grown up in front of the boob tube. This is true not only in the literal sense, but is the perfect symbolic representation of our general condition, both within and without Christendom. We have been insulated and sheltered, and have not gotten the full brunt and force of life as it is. Reality has been so filtered and refined that we have not understood it in its totality. We need God to open our eyes.

"And when they had laid many stripes upon them . . ." I praise the Lord for His discretion; only He knows the number of strokes that "many" refers to. In the second letter to the Corinthians, Paul wrote that he had received thirty-nine stripes on five different occasions (2 Corinthians 11:24). Forty lashes was the maximum punishment by whipping prescribed by Jewish law (Deuteronomy 25:1-3). It was traditional in the synagogues to stop one short of forty to be sure of not going over the limit. Such was the practice of Paul's own Jewish people; the Philippian Gentiles who laid many stripes upon them, beating them with rods, were under no obligation to remain within that law's boundary.

Can you picture Paul and Silas, their clothes stripped from them, publicly humiliated in the market place? Then, the first lash—the sound of it alone is enough to make you sick. CRACK. You see the ugly red welt appear as that rod comes crashing down against the naked flesh . . . and there are yet many more stripes to go. As those rods keep swishing and cracking, what was first red has been turning somewhat blue—CRACK—turning sickly green—CRACK—the skin is rent—CRACK—those sticks cut right into the open flesh all the way to the bone . . . and we have not yet counted ten. When those men were finally cast into the inner prison, they were as pathetic a sight as one could ever imagine.

Wherever we shall touch this present world system by the power of the Spirit, we shall be brought before the rulers and magistrates in the market place, where the action is. "Katz, you sound so much like the radical you once were." I am not referring to communism, socialism, or capitalism, but to the entire network ruled over by the prince of darkness, that system which plays upon the lusts and ambitions of men. If you rock it, challenge it, and set captives free by the power of the Holy Spirit, you will not fail to elicit strong reaction. It is clear why tongues are being torn out of Christian heads behind the Iron Curtain; their very existence, lives committed to standing in God's truth, constitutes a dangerous threat to the established order.

There is a principle of God here: we shall suffer in this world in exact proportion to the degree of obedience we render to Him. He will call us from faith to faith, or more pointedly, from death to death. That is why the love of many will grow cold. Not many have a stomach for that kind of service.

"Gee, you used to be groovy, Art. Now you're a wet blanket, man. I thought that you loved the Jesus movement. Didn't we have great times witnessing and playing guitars and singing songs?" Don't misunderstand me. I am not knocking that. There is value in it. There are many, however, who were having a great time who are not going to be around in that last hour. The forces are going to be reduced, for not everyone will be willing to wear the crown of thorns which must precede the crown of glory.

"These men, being Jews, do exceedingly trouble our city." You do not have to be born Jewish to be this kind of "Jew." Such a one as this is made only by an operation of the Spirit, a circumcision, not of the flesh, but of the heart. The "Jew" who can exceedingly trouble our cities is one who esteems the praise of God more than the praise of men.

I was in Zurich recently, and, on my first day there, I took a walk through the city. It was the last word in refinement, in modern ingenuity, in human attainment, in things to wear, in things to possess. There was an array of cars of every shape, size, and make. Women were adorned in jewels and fur coats. Amidst the unspeakable luxury and wealth, I saw people walking as corpses everywhere. I returned to the apartment in which I was staying, stretched out like a dead man on the floor, and convulsively sobbed and gushed like a child.

When will Zurich be shaken? Geneva? Berlin? Frankfort? Paris? Moscow? London? New York? Los Angeles? In every great city, men are moving to their doom without the slightest awareness that they are on such a course. God is looking for "Jews" who will exceedingly trouble cities. Our cities are already being shaken for Satan by those who deal in bombs, crime, rebellion and pornography. Where are the "Jews" of God, under the power of His Spirit, ready to shake cities for Christ? Where are the mature men and women who, when they are called to the chief cities by a heavenly vision, will set forth with a straight course, expecting neither a wreath nor a plaque from the hands of the princes of this world, but only, if need be, suffering, humiliation, and shame?

And the Prisoners Heard Them
Perhaps some of you have been to Rome and have visited the cell in which Paul spent his latter years. It is similar to the one in which he and Silas were incarcerated in Philippi. During a trip to Italy, I stopped off at that place.

It is a black hole which glistens with sweat in the heat of the day. The smell of human urine and feces still exists in that place though it has not been used as a prison for centuries. Imagine what it smelled like when it was used. In that stench, rats and vermin would scurry about, and the groans of prisoners would be heard from other parts of the prison. It was a hellish inferno.

I am the kind of a guy who has trouble sitting still in a charismatic meeting for more than a half hour without getting itchy, moving, stretching, trying to get more comfortable (as we say in Yiddish, I have no *zitzflaisch*).

Paul and Silas, while in unspeakable pain, their backs hanging in shreds, had their feet bound in the stocks; they could not even alter their position.

How would most of us respond to finding ourselves in such a situation? We would be tempted to say, "Oh God, where did I go wrong? How did I miss it? I thought I was obedient to the heavenly vision, but look at me now." We say this kind of thing about much lesser difficulties. You got stood up on a date; you didn't get the income tax return that you thought you deserved; you were not applauded and approved in the way that you had hoped for; *it simply is not going the way you like it*. Those two first-century disciples, in a condition of suffering that eclipses anything that we have experienced for the Lord, responded differently:

> And at midnight Paul and Silas prayed, and sang praises unto God.
>
> Acts 16:25a

We are circled about by an invisible cloud of witnesses, men who, throughout the ages, have prayed and sung praises to God in the midst of their adversity. They are looking upon us, waiting for us to finish the race that is set before us, that we might rejoice together.

We have made a big deal about praise in the charismatic movement. It has almost become a technique and a formula. "Get 'em up out of their seats; get 'em to lift their hands above their heads; get 'em to sing those choruses over and over. If we get them excited enough, we'll have a great meeting."

The gifts of the Spirit have nothing to do with methodologies of manipulation; they are *holy, holy, holy*. God has given divine enablements for every contingency and every need at the end of the ages. Men speak of the Spirit of

God as if He has come to enhance our denominations and spice up our meetings. Have a reverence for Him. We have been given *holy* provisions for *holy* tasks by the *Holy* Spirit.

"And at midnight Paul and Silas prayed, and sang praises unto God." If, during my darkest fit of atheism, just the page with this glorious verse on it had floated down the street, I believe that, after picking it up and reading it, I would have fallen on my face before God and worshiped Him; I would have known that no men can praise and worship God in such crisis, adversity and suffering *except* there be a Holy Spirit.

We can read about martyrs through the ages who were flung to the lions, roasted on coals, and burned at the stake, who sang praises until their voices were gone. In that express moment, God endows His children with a special dispensation of grace, an intimacy with Him in the fellowship of His sufferings that enables them to do more than endure. By this heavenly miracle, men can gloriously testify to the world about the reality of the Messiah Jesus and the God of our fathers in the hour of their cruelest suffering. To this hour we are being called.

During his third missionary journey, Paul, in his words of parting to the Ephesian elders at Miletus, exemplified the attitude of heart that God is seeking to establish in the hearts of His people.

> And now, behold, I go bound in the spirit unto Jerusalem, not knowing the things that shall befall me there:
>
> Save that the Holy Ghost witnesseth in every city, saying that bonds and afflictions abide [await] me.
>
> But none of these things move me, neither count I my life dear unto myself, so that I might finish my course with joy, and the ministry, which I have

received of the Lord Jesus, to testify the gospel of
the grace of God.

Acts 20:22-24

A Yugoslavian brother once said to me, with earnest hope
and humility, "Art, maybe God has reserved for me the
honor of wearing a martyr's crown." Such men as these are
not fashioned in a moment.

This is not a time for pampering and soft indulgence. God
desires to raise up an army and to prepare us as spiritual
soldiers. We need to become a disciplined people who know
what it means to deny our fleshly appetites and to submit to
the testings and shapings at God's hand.

Too many of us still strongly object whenever something
impinges upon our flesh. I have seen believers balk at the
prospect of going to the dentist. As long as our priorities
remain fleshly, we shall be a people who shrink from pain and
run from suffering.

As Christ's disciples, each of us is confronted by the same
fundamental decision. The writer to the Hebrews clearly
delineates the nature of this choice in the example of Moses:

> By faith Moses, when he was come to years,
> refused to be called the son of Pharaoh's daughter;
> *Choosing rather to suffer affliction with the
> people of God, than to enjoy the pleasures of sin
> for a season;*
> Esteeming the reproach of Christ greater
> riches than the treasures in Egypt: for he had
> respect unto the recompense of the reward.
> By faith he forsook Egypt, not fearing the
> wrath of the king: for he endured, as seeing him
> who is invisible.

Hebrews 11:24-27
(our italics)

I am a rather simple-minded man who sees everything in polarities: light and darkness, good and evil, flesh and Spirit, and so on. The same two alternatives that existed for Moses exist for the children of the Lord at the end of the ages—suffering affliction with the people of God or enjoying the pleasures of sin for a season. There shall not be a third course.

We have considered only the first part of that twenty-fifth verse of Acts 16: "And at midnight Paul and Silas prayed, and sang praises unto God." The most beautiful and glorious part follows:

> . . . and the prisoners heard them.
>
> Acts 16:25b

I do not have the slightest doubt that, when I get to heaven, I am going to see every prisoner there who heard Paul and Silas.

Why do we come home spent and depressed from our evangelistic campaigns? Nothing much seems to be accomplished in the eternal realm. Our words seem so often like water off the proverbial duck's back: no penetration. How many times have we flung ourselves down in exhaustion, crushed with a sense of futility, and cried out, "Oh God, what does it take?"

It is going to take more than correct words, something more than glibly and unctuously delivered Scripture quotations. I believe with all my heart that our final end-time witness shall be our real joy in God and our praise and worship of Him *in the midst of adversity and affliction.* "And the prisoners heard them."

God allowed His Hebrew children Shadrach, Meshach, and Abednego to go through a fiery furnace. They came out of it without a single hair singed and without even the smell of smoke on their bodies. I believe that our God Who changeth not shall deal with His children in the same wondrous way at the end of the ages. I do not expect that we shall be conveniently raptured away when the going gets hot. We shall pass safely through the fire, and our passing through shall be a revelation of the glorious reality of God to those who are suffering everywhere about us. Filled with the Holy Spirit, we shall not cease to praise God and sing of our love for Him; and the prisoners shall hear us.

Liberty

> And suddenly there was a great earthquake, so that the foundations of the prison were shaken: and immediately all the doors were opened, and every one's bands were loosed.
>
> Acts 16:26

"Oh, Art, what a wonderful coincidence. Isn't that strange? In the very moment that they were praising God, an earthquake came. Talk about coincidences. And look, look, everyone's bands fell, and the doors burst open, and—" Coincidence, my foot. God inhabits the praises of His people (Psalm 22:3), "and where the Spirit of the Lord is, there is liberty" (2 Corinthians 3:17b).

Our God is the God of truth, and He does not and never shall dwell in praises that are not authentic or that issue forth from our lips only in the absence of crisis. It is one thing to praise God while you are comfortable, clothed, sheltered, and fed, when every need is provided for. Can you, however, praise Him when everything has gone wrong, when you are alone, you don't understand why, and He is not quick to explain? That is the kind of praise that opens prison doors and shakes foundations.

Many of you are waiting for your circumstances to improve. God, however, is waiting for you to open your mouth and praise Him in your present affliction and deprivation. Paul and Silas did not accidentally stumble into prison. Our Lord knew from the first that their obedience to Him was going to result in suffering and humiliation. They praised God and rejoiced that they were counted worthy to suffer shame for Christ's name.

We need to have the foundations of our lives so shaken that we may sing of our love and thankfulness to God in the depths of our crises. When those two men worshiped the Holy One of Israel from that stinking cell, "immediately all the doors were opened, and every one's bands were loosed." There was perfect liberty. The Spirit of the Lord had intervened.

> And the keeper of the prison awaking out of his sleep . . .
>
> Acts 16:27a

The awakening out of sleep has ever been and must always be the first step in real conversion. About a decade later, Paul would write to the church at Ephesus:

> Wherefore he saith, Awake thou that sleepest, and arise from the dead, and Christ shall give thee light.
>
> Ephesians 5:14

The keeper of that prison is the perfect picture of worldly security and respectability. He is the first-century Philippian equivalent of today's nominal Christian who seeks only to keep his nose clean before the eyes of men, goes to church every Sunday, and waits for his retirement and his pension—"all this and heaven too." Can't you just see him outside that prison, soundly slumbering, and clutching the keys?

The jailer, who appeared to be a free man, was actually more bound than Paul and Silas in that inner prison. Fearful of endangering the security of his position, intimidated by the threats of the world, he was manifestly bound, though he held the keys. What will it take to awaken the prison keepers of our own generation? Nothing less than an earthquake.

> And the keeper of the prison awaking out of his sleep, and seeing the prison doors open, he drew out his sword, and would have killed himself, supposing that the prisoners had been fled.
> But Paul cried with a loud voice, saying, Do thyself no harm: for we are all here.
>
> Acts 16:27, 28

"Don't get excited; we're here. We're not going anywhere. Why should we? We weren't prisoners before and we're not prisoners now; to be free in Christ is to be free indeed." If obedience to the Lord has brought you to a place behind bars, you are seated in heaven. Richard Wurmbrand, a Jewish believer who spent thirteen years in communist prison camps, said that when he left prison it was like coming *down* from the mountaintop experience. Remember again that other Hebrew prisoner:

> And Joseph's master took him, and put him into the prison, a place where the king's prisoners were bound: and he was there in the prison.

146

But the Lord was with Joseph, and shewed him mercy, and gave him favour in the sight of the keeper of the prison.

Genesis 39:20,21
(our italics)

"The steps of a good man are ordered by the Lord" (Psalm 37:23a). Wheresoever God has brought you, to whatever circumstance, however unpleasant, however much it contradicts your own intentions, however trapped you may appear, *you are free*. If He is with you and in you in that cell, it matters not whether the doors are opened or closed. "If the Son therefore shall make you free, ye shall be free indeed" (John 8:36).

"Do thyself no harm: for we are all here." How did Paul know that the jailer was ready to kill himself, when he obviously could not see him? He did not see him by the natural eye, but by the eye of the Spirit through the gift of knowledge. He shouted out and saved that man's life. We may have thought that the gifts of the Spirit were simply to dazzle us and tickle our ears at church meetings. They shall, however, make the difference between life and death in these last days.

Repent Ye, and Believe the Gospel

I was very well-meaning as a young high school teacher; I wanted to do such a smash-up job and be everything that teachers were not for me when I was an adolescent. I dished out all kinds of information to those kids, the best that I had to offer, but it was going completely over their heads.

There was an important lesson wrapped up in that experience that I had to learn the hard way: *it is absolutely stupid to give people answers for questions that they have not yet asked.*

> Then he [the keeper of the prison] called for a
> light, and sprang in, and came trembling, and fell
> down before Paul and Silas,
>
> And brought them out, and said, Sirs, what
> must I do to be saved?
>
> Acts 16:29, 30

By the eye of the Spirit we can see the question burning in someone's heart, or, as in this case, we may be directly asked, "Sirs, what must I do to be saved?"

We have been cheapening the name of Jesus Christ. He is not exalted by our attempts to cram that precious name down the throats of those who do not even have the faintest concept of what salvation is or of their desperate need for it. Our function is not to give glib answers for questions that have not been raised, but to be instruments through whom the Holy Spirit may raise the proper questions in the hearts of men.

There is no methodology, no prescribed format of so-called "witnessing." Jesus says to His disciples:

> Ye are the light of the world. A city that is set on
> an hill cannot be hid.
>
> Neither do men light a candle, and put it under a
> bushel, but on a candlestick; and it giveth light
> unto all that are in the house.
>
> Let your light so shine before men, that they
> may see your good works, and glorify your Father
> which is in heaven.
>
> Matthew 5:14-16

As we learn to rest in the Lord, His very presence shall bring men to a divine discontent with their prosperity, their reputations, their culture, their neat ethical systems, their whole lives; the Spirit of God shall reveal that "all have sinned, and come short of the glory of God" (Romans 3:23). There is not a soul who can receive such a message by dry verbal proclamation; when they see His glory in your face and feel His touch upon their hearts, they shall call for light, and, trembling, cry out, "What must I do to be saved?"

> And they said, Believe on the Lord Jesus Christ, and thou shalt be saved, and thy house.
> Acts 16:31

Paul and Silas were speaking about much more than a notional assent to an intellectual concept. The Amplified Bible translates this verse:

> And they answered, Believe in and on the Lord Jesus Christ—that is, give yourself up to Him, take yourself out of your own keeping and entrust yourself into His keeping, and you will be saved; [and this applies both to] you and your household as well.

To believe on Christ is to cast your whole life upon Him, to make Him the life of your life. *There is no real believing without repentance.* The earliest recorded preaching of Jesus delivers the same simple and powerful message:

> Now after that John was put in prison, Jesus came into Galilee, preaching the gospel of the kingdom of God,
> And saying, The time is fulfilled, and the kingdom of God is at hand: repent ye, and believe the gospel.
> Mark 1:14, 15

149

There are a lot of people who have confessed the name of Jesus who have not yet repented; I have great reservations about, not only their conversion, but about their salvation itself. *"Repent* ye, and believe the gospel." Believing is a function of repentance. The unrepentant heart cannot receive the foolish things which God has given us to believe. The gospel of Jesus Christ is absolutely mind-boggling; it contradicts every kind of human wisdom and natural understanding.

We cannot expect the sophisticated, convoluted minds and the proud, self-assured hearts of this world to believe that God Himself laid aside His glory, took upon Himself the form of flesh, and became a Jew who was born in a stable; that He lived a life of obscurity and came forth in His thirtieth year, had a three-year public ministry during which He suffered reproach, and had not a place to lay His head; that He was nailed to a cross, where He poured out His blood unto death, out of love for those who betrayed Him; that His body was resurrected from the dead and He has risen to the right hand of the Father in heaven; that, if you believe this and take that blood of Jesus, the Lamb of God, and apply it to the doorpost and lintel of your heart and life, death will pass over you; you shall be saved. "Come on, Katz. Knock it off. What do you think I am? Some kind of fool? Only an idiot could believe fables like that!" Truly there is nothing more foolish, nothing more beggarly, that we can ever present to a stiffnecked humanity:

> For the preaching of the cross is to them that perish foolishness; but unto us which are saved it is the power of God.
>
> 1 Corinthians 1:18

Before I knew God, I was like a dead man stalking

Europe. I had no understanding of the word repentance, but, toward the end, I had, in effect, repented; I had turned away from this world's wisdom and its way. In brokenness and nothingness, I had become a candidate for the hearing of the still small voice of God. It is our function, in the power of the Spirit, to challenge men and to bring them to that place, that they might cry out to God as David did after he was visited by the prophet Nathan:

> Deliver me from bloodguiltiness, O God, thou God of my salvation: and my tongue shall sing aloud of thy righteousness.
> O Lord, open thou my lips; and my mouth shall shew forth thy praise.
> For thou desirest not sacrifice; else would I give it: thou delightest not in burnt offering.
> The sacrifices of God are a broken spirit: a broken and a contrite heart, O God, thou wilt not despise.
>
> Psalm 51:14-17

That I May Win Christ

> And they spake unto him the word of the Lord, and to all that were in his house.
> And he took them the same hour of the night, and washed their stripes; and was baptized, he and all his, straightway.
> And when he had brought them into his house, he set meat before them, and rejoiced, believing in God with all his house.
>
> Acts 16:32-34

That prison keeper was delivered from the power of darkness that keeps men fearfully clutching the keys of worldly security, and transferred by the heavenly Father into the kingdom of His beloved Son. He and his family, a few prisoners, Lydia and her household, and the demoniacal woman who was set free became the Body of Christ in Philippi. That Body was born because men were willing to follow the example of their Lord in suffering and in the shedding of their blood. "So then death worketh in us," Paul wrote, "but life in you" (2 Corinthians 4:12). This is the way of God, and there is no way to walk in it except by the Holy Spirit.

In His last public discourse, Jesus looked toward His imminent death on the cross:

> And Jesus answered them, saying, The hour is come, that the Son of man should be glorified.
>
> Verily, verily, I say unto you, Except a corn of wheat fall into the ground and die, it abideth alone: but if it die, it bringeth forth much fruit.
>
> He that loveth his life shall lose it; and he that hateth his life in this world shall keep it unto life eternal.
>
> If any man serve me, let him follow me; and where I am, there shall also my servant be: if any man serve me, him will my Father honour.
>
> John 12:23-26

That mind which was in Christ Jesus was also in His servants, Paul and Silas, for they were filled with the Spirit of the Lord. In his letter to those Philippian believers, Paul enumerated the natural attributes that he had once depended upon and boasted about (Philippians 3:4-6). Like every consecrated believer, however, Paul was brought to the place of having "no confidence in the flesh" (Philippians 3:3). He had seen the pearl of great price, and had given up all for the sake of Christ. May God open our eyes and our hearts, that we may, in freedom and in truth, say amen to that statement of faith and love which our Lord's apostle wrote to that band of saints in Philippi:

But what things were gain to me, those I counted loss for Christ.

Yea doubtless, and I count all things but loss for the excellency of the knowledge of Christ Jesus my Lord: for whom I have suffered the loss of all things, and do count them but dung, that I may win Christ,

And be found in him, not having mine own righteousness, which is of the law, but that which is through the faith of Christ, the righteousness which is of God by faith:

That I may know him, and the power of his resurrection, and the fellowship of his sufferings, being made conformable unto his death;

If by any means I might attain unto the resurrection of the dead.

Not as though I had already attained, either were already perfect: but I follow after, if that I may apprehend that for which also I am apprehended of Christ Jesus.

Brethren, I count not myself to have apprehended: but this one thing I do, forgetting those things which are behind, and reaching forth unto those things which are before,

I press toward the mark for the prize of the high calling of God in Christ Jesus.

Philippians 3:7-14

CHAPTER 4

Be Ye Perfect:
The Sabbath of God's Rest

Thus saith the Lord, Stand ye in the ways, and see, and ask for the old paths, where is the good way, and walk therein, and ye shall find rest for your souls. But they said, We will not walk therein.

Jeremiah 6:16

Christ, Our Wisdom and Knowledge

In 1968, the ministry of speaking on university campuses began for me at the University of Illinois, in Urbana. I was in over my head, beyond my experience, maturity, wisdom, and knowledge, but I was constrained of God to go. When I arrived at the campus, I found that my associates there had fashioned little strips, and had glued them all over the place. On each of them, three words were joined together as one: KATZISCOMING.

I cannot express how mortified and embarrassed I was to see that. I hated anything that celebrated personalities or the names of men, and I really took issue with the committee that had decided upon that course. They promised me that the Lord had clearly directed them. They were sure that if they had advertised some kind of abstract gospel meeting no one would have come. A new question arose in my heart: "Are you so dead and hid with Christ in God that it makes absolutely no difference to you whether your name is used or is not?" I knew that God had cornered me and that He Himself was ordaining the use of my name. I told the committee that I would go along with it.

That university was known at that time for all sorts of radical activities, and had recently been visited by state troops and militia during a student riot. Every day at one o'clock at the Student Union center, radicals would take the microphone, spew forth filth, and give invitations to violence. It was right there that I was scheduled to speak at the first of eight days of meetings. Before my conversion, I had been a Marxist of the old vintage and did not even have a vocabulary in common with that generation of radicals. But the Lord was calling.

I remember going into a little football huddle with the other Christians and, clinging together, we asked the Lord's blessing. The prayer ended, the circle broke, and I found

156

myself before the microphone—alone. Standing there with my face sticking out, I had never felt more weak, beggarly, or ill-equipped. I looked across a room which was jammed with angry and contentious students. The fate of the next eight days was hanging on this initial encounter.

As I started to speak, I looked straight to the back of the room and my eyes fell upon a particular individual. He had a face that was the epitome of every wise-alecky and cynical opposition to God that this world can produce; he was a perfect type of the Art Katz that I was only a few short years before. When I saw that guy licking his lips and rubbing his hands in gleeful anticipation, I knew that he was going to be trouble.

Having finished my short presentation, I foolishly opened for questions. Of course, his hand was the first to go up. Elbowing his friends and smirking, his whole demeanor seemed to say, "Okay, guys, I've got this under control. I'll put this guy Katz down from the beginning and that'll be the end of the whole ball game." With a voice that was dripping with mockery, he said, "Mr. Katz, do you believe in hell?"

I was completely taken aback. It was a question for which I was totally unprepared. Once again, I found myself without a neat little booklet, alphabetically indexed: "H—hell." The Word of God is explicit about His provision for His children:

> But of him are ye in Christ Jesus, who of God is made unto us wisdom . . . in whom are hid all the treasures of wisdom and knowledge.
> 1 Corinthians 1:30a
> Colossians 2:3

Do you believe that? Will you believe it, not only when you are sitting safely and comfortably in the company of the saints, but also when your face is sticking out before a hostile audience, and it is a matter of life and death for them and for you?

A lot of us are in an infantile spiritual condition because we have not lived by faith like that. "The just shall *live* by faith" (Romans 1:17b). Faith is more than giving mental agreement to the things which God speaks. It is living it in a moment of crisis, where we affirm with our whole life, "though he slay me, yet will I trust in him" (Job 13:15a). That is the acid test. I knew, as I stood before those leering faces, that, if God was *not* made unto me wisdom and knowledge, I would be intimidated, humiliated, and vanquished.

As I looked at my inquisitor, I was reviewing something silently in my spirit with the Lord: "You got me here. This wasn't my idea. I wasn't seeking for any brilliant university ministry, and I'm not advancing any career. You prompted me to come, and, Lord, You and I know how wholly unqualified I am, so now *You* give this guy answer." (That is the way this Jewish man sometimes speaks to his God.)

Here is what then came out of my mouth: "Sir, I have always had a devout respect for words. Even when I was an atheist, I remember flushing with a kind of embarrassment and indignation when some kid in a junior high school class called a girl a whore. It made me rankle that that jerk was using a word indiscriminately because it made him feel like some kind of sophisticate. Words are not to be bandied about lightly. They are powerful things and can be holy or profane. They can bring life or can cripple or kill.

"There is another, about whom we read in the Scriptures, who had a profound reverence for words—Jesus Himself. He it is Who said that we shall be accountable for every idle word we speak. He never spoke one word idly, and there is not another person in all the Scriptures who has spoken more prolifically about hell than He. He is the One Who spoke of 'wailing and gnashing of teeth,' 'casting into outer darkness,' 'the lake of fire,' 'torment,' and 'the fire that shall not be quenched.' Sir, it behooves you to hear *His* statements about hell lest you find yourself, more quickly than you think, to be standing before Him, your knees turning to jelly, with your foolish question which you've asked to embarrass His servant played back in your hearing much too late for you to use it."

Like a punctured balloon, that proud man deflated, shrivelled up, and seemed to just blow away. It was not Katz who had come up with something humanly clever to save the day. God Himself, in whom are hid all the treasures of wisdom and knowledge, gave an answer which was *perfect*.

Be Thou Perfect

Jesus said:

> Be ye therefore perfect, even as your Father which is in heaven is perfect.
>
> Matthew 5:48

Perfect? I used to wonder, when I would read that passage as a young believer, whether God was speaking in approximate terms, was goading us, was speaking tongue-in-cheek, or actually meant it. The spirit of the world is entirely contrary to the Lord's command. How frequently have we heard such expressions as "human, all too human," and "I'm only human, you know." We Christians even hide behind such statements as "I'm a sinner saved by grace," which, true as it is in itself, is often used to imply that we are virtually *required* to sin day by day. If we stumble and fall, shall we make stumbling and falling our goal? We who have been born again by the Spirit of God need not conduct our lives by human standards or resources:

> And they that are Christ's have crucified the
> flesh with the affections and lusts.
> If we live in the Spirit, let us also walk in the
> Spirit.
>
> Galatians 5:24, 25

It is *only in Him* that we can ever walk perfectly, for He alone is perfect.

In the first verse of Chapter 17 of Genesis, we read,

> And when Abram was ninety years old and
> nine, the Lord appeared to Abram, and said unto
> him, I am the Almighty God; walk before me, and
> *be thou perfect.*
>
> (our italics)

Of all the times that the Lord has spoken, this is the first time that He has described Himself as "the Almighty God." There has never been a syllable emitted from the mouth of God that has been mere happenstance. In His relationship with His people and with Abraham in particular, He has described Himself in different ways at different times, never wasting a word or speaking haphazardly. That is why we can depend upon *living* "by every word that proceedeth out of the mouth of God" (Matthew 4:4; Deuteronomy 8:3).

Why does it please God to introduce Himself in this way? "I am the Almighty God." It is because, in the same breath, He says, "Walk before me and be thou perfect." This is not a chance coupling of two phrases; it is a perfect statement of God, utterly logical, reasonable, and necessary. To call one to perfection and to a walk before God and not before men requires from that one who is called a complete confidence that the God who has invited him will also supply every necessary means. That is why His almightiness is so important. Abram was in his ninety-ninth year when this monumental word of the Lord came to him. Which one of us is strong enough, wise enough, deep enough, brave enough, or loving enough to be perfect and walk before God? However young you are, however full of human energy and good intentions you are, as far as the end-time purposes of God are concerned, you are infirm and feeble . . . ninety-nine years old.

The call of God to Abram and the call of God to us is *a call to the impossible*. That's why I love it. It far eclipses religion. I am not asking my Jewish people to leave "country-club Judaism" or "ceremonial Judaism" or "sterile Judaism" and come to a more prosperous alternative. I have never asked them to leave a Jewish religion and enter a gentile one. That is not the question at all. They are being invited to leave the "Judaisms" of the world by whatever name. Religionists of all description, from Buddhists to Methodists, are being asked to come to Abrahamic faith and commitment and to a supernatural relationship with God by which they shall receive the empowering and the enablement of God to walk in a way that transcends anything human.

For we believers to say "I'm only human" is a cop-out and a complete revelation of how much we have misunderstood what it is to which God has called us. We have not clearly seen the miraculous fact: "Christ in [us], the hope of glory" (Colossians 1:27). He Who is the Head of all principalities and powers and in Whom all the fulness of the Godhead dwells bodily is the same One Who dwells in us by the Spirit, and *through Him* we receive all the things that pertain to godliness and to life, that we can walk *perfectly* before our God.

Getting By

The purposes of God are so complex and so interwoven in a world-wide tapestry that there is nothing that happens anywhere on the face of the earth that does not touch His workings elsewhere. What the Lord is doing in Germany, for example, shall directly affect conditions in Israel. He has given me an enormous burden for Germany. "But, Art," you say, "I thought you were called to the Jews?" I am. Do you remember the old adage, "The way to a man's heart is through his stomach"? God has shown me that the way to Israel is through Germany, that He has a purpose for the Body of Christ in Germany in His ultimate end-time intentions for the Holy Land.

Who could have thought of such a thing? Who would have thought of such a circuitous route to accomplish the purposes of God? It appears to us to be a needless distraction; we are prone to take the quickest, easiest, and seemingly most direct way. It has never been more incumbent upon any generation than ours, however, to understand God's call: "Be ye therefore perfect, even as your Father which is in heaven is perfect . . . walk before me and be thou perfect." If our hearts are intent upon seeing the Lord's perfect will fulfilled, He shall provide the means for its fulfillment in our lives. He is the Lord God Almighty, and He looks upon the heart.

What William Law wrote in eighteenth-century England is an important word to those who call themselves Christians today:

> You will perhaps insist that all people fall short of the perfection of the gospel, and therefore you feel justified in your failings. But this is saying nothing to the purpose. For the question is not whether gospel perfection can be fully attained,

162

but whether you come as near it as a sincere intention and careful diligence can carry you through faith in Christ. If your defects in piety, humility, and charity are owing to your negligence and lack of sincere intention to be as eminent in these virtues as the saving life of Christ and the power of the Holy Spirit can make a redeemed sinner, then you have left yourself without excuse. And may it not be that you have stopped short of the terms of the gospel? Can you really call yourself a follower of Christ without at least *intending* to follow Him all the way? [7]

We are only too eager to receive second best. If something works, if it's utilitarian, if we can get by, that is enough. When I was a high-school teacher, the kids would come to my desk at the beginning of each semester and say, "Mr. Katz, what is the minimum amount I need to do in order to get by?" We are a get-by people; we have lived and grown up in that mentality and we have brought it right into the kingdom of God with us.

I will never forget my introduction to a fellowship of precious German believers in Jerusalem. They had invited another Jewish brother and myself to dinner at their residence in the basement of a Lutheran church in the old city. We were hot, sweaty, and tired after touring all day with a little group. I needed to wash up and asked our hostess if she had a towel. She said yes, opened up the towel closet, and, as I stood there, my jaw dropped. What a glorious sight!

"Katz," you say, "what are you waxing so ecstatic about towels for? I didn't see you as a dry goods man." It wasn't the towels. It was the *order* in which the towels were kept. The symmetry, precision, and perfection in that linen closet were staggering to behold. It was not the usual slipshod, jammed-in kind of a thing with which we Americans are familiar. The condition of that closet was symptomatic of more than cultural differences; it was but one manifestation of the dominion of God's Spirit in that place. *Our God is the God of order and perfection.* I experienced a tranquillity, a peace, and a presence of God in that fellowship that night which has remained with me still, and has spoiled me for any lesser thing.

There is so much that is shoddy in our "charismatic" life, so much hotshot nonsense, noise, and ballyhoo. "But, Art, I'm getting by. I'm not in deep carnal sin, I'm not fornicating. I'm only human." If that is the condition you desire, then that is the condition in which you shall remain. As long as you are willing and content to receive second best, my God will never press the perfect thing upon you; but if there is a cry in your heart, "Lord, I want to be perfect and walk before you," He shall bring you to that perfection, day by day, through the same process by which He brought Abraham.

Don't expect it to be pleasant, easy, and convenient.

> Now the Lord had said unto Abram, Get thee out of thy country, and from thy kindred, and from thy father's house, unto a land that I will shew thee.
>
> Genesis 12:1

God's initial call to Abraham was a call to a radical commitment *and* to a wrenching separation from all that was familiar and dear. From that day on, he was shaped by God's hand through trial and error, going down south into Egypt, mortifications, embarrassments: adventures from faith unto faith (or, we could just as well say, from death unto death).

164

The supreme test came years later:

> And it came to pass after these things, that God
> did tempt Abraham, and said unto him, Abraham:
> and he said, Behold, here I am.
>
> And he said, Take now thy son, thine only son
> Isaac, whom thou lovest, and get thee into the
> land of Moriah; and offer him there for a burnt
> offering upon one of the mountains which I will tell
> thee of.
>
> Genesis 22:1, 2

Isaac, the long-awaited miraculous fruit of Sarah's barren
womb, was Abraham's delight and was more precious to him
than his own life, yet we hear not one objection, not one
complaint toward the God who had given him the command.
Might not some of us have argued, "But Lord, didn't you
promise that from this seed there was to be blessing for all
nations?" Our temptation would be to get by with an easier
and more "humane" alternative, but

> Abraham rose up early in the morning, and
> saddled his ass, and took two of his young men
> with him, and Isaac his son, and clave the wood for
> the burnt offering, and rose up, and went unto the
> place of which God had told him.
>
> Genesis 22:3

God called him, and, with a quiet and meek spirit, a true
spirit of submissiveness, he arose and went to the mountain
and built the altar upon which he was to lay Isaac (verse 9).
That father would have much preferred to lay his own body
across the altar than his beloved son's. God knows how to put
the finger on that thing which is most dear to us, that His

pre-eminence (or its absence) in our hearts might be revealed. When God saw Abraham stretch forth his hand and raise the knife above his son to slay him (verse 10), He knew that the act was virtually performed; His servant had fully intended to come down with that blade. How blessed must the Lord have been to gaze upon His servant whose heart was perfect toward Him.

> And the angel of the Lord called unto him out of heaven, and said, Abraham, Abraham: and he said, Here am I.
> And he said, Lay not thine hand upon the lad, neither do thou any thing unto him: for now I know that thou fearest God, seeing thou hast not withheld thy son, thine only son from me.
>
> Genesis 22:11, 12

To have a heart that is perfect before the Lord is to hold *nothing* back from Him. Getting by is not enough. We are called to the faith of Abraham:

> Know ye therefore that they which are of faith, the same are the children of Abraham.
> And if ye be Christ's, then are ye Abraham's seed, and heirs according to the promise.
>
> Galatians 3:7, 29

There shall be a moment for each of us, maybe several such moments, when God is going to call us to raise the knife upon that Isaac which is more dear to us than perhaps our own life. If we have ignored the Lord's first two commands ("Get thee out . . . ," "Walk before me, and be thou perfect"), calls to utter separation and devotion, we may find ourselves powerless for the fulfillment of His third.

166

We shall neither enjoy nor spread Christian blessing except as the fruit of an Abrahamic faith, for "they which be of faith are blessed with faithful Abraham" (Galatians 3:9). Our obedient ancestor received God's great mercy when the Lord supplied a ram to be offered in the place of Isaac (verse 13); through the shedding of that animal's blood, God's perfect justice was satisfied, the life of Abraham's only son was spared, and the future existence of the nation of Israel was secured. So much more, however, than just a natural progeny was granted to Abraham; to him and to his spiritual seed were given all the promises of Messianic blessing.

And the angel of the Lord called unto Abraham out of heaven the second time,

And said, By myself have I sworn, saith the Lord, for because thou hast done this thing, and hast not withheld thy son, thine only son:

That in blessing I will bless thee, and in multiplying I will multiply thy seed as the stars of the heaven, and as the sand which is upon the sea shore; and thy seed shall possess the gate of his enemies;

And in thy seed shall all the nations of the earth be blessed; because thou hast obeyed my voice.

Genesis 22:15-18

Now to Abraham and his seed were the promises made. He saith not, And to seeds, as of many; but as of one, And to thy seed, which is Christ.

Galatians 3:16

For as the body is one, and hath many members, and all the members of that one body, being many, are one body: so also is Christ.

For by one Spirit are we all baptized into one body, whether we be Jews or Gentiles, whether we be bond or free; and have been all made to drink into one Spirit.

1 Corinthians 12:12, 13

The Good and the Perfect

In 1974, I received a letter from a young man in California who wrote that he was a seeker after truth, had studied philosophy at the Sorbonne, had been involved in a multitude of causes, ideologies, cults, Eastern religions, you name it. He had recently been witnessed to by some Christians and had been given a copy of *Ben Israel* in which he found a kindred soul. He wrote that he was ready to fly to New York, that we might discuss the great questions of life. I hastily wrote him a letter, in which I said, in effect, "Take it easy, guy, I don't know who you are, you're into the occult . . . I'm not so quick to invite you under my roof."

Not long after, he gave me a long distance telephone call: he still wanted to come. "Look," I said, "I'm going to be in California in a couple of weeks. Why don't we just rendezvous there, and, while you're waiting, why don't you visit a family with whom I received the baptism in the Holy Spirit. They can, I know, answer many of your questions." He agreed to visit my old friends, the Fultzes.

Two weeks later, I arrived in California and discovered that they had led him to the Lord and that he had received the baptism in the Holy Spirit. After years of groping in darkness he had finally seen the Light, and he felt ready to go and proclaim to all the world the life-giving message. It turned out that we would spend the next ten days together traveling from city to city and from meeting to meeting in his van.

It was not the kind of discipling situation in which I was laying down the precepts of the faith in a systematic way. I was, however, using the existential material and circumstances that God was supplying to give him understanding. One morning, after just having started out, he picked up a hitchhiker. As I watched my young friend's face, I had a witness in my heart: "God is doing something." How precious is that sense during the unfolding of an event: "This is God."

Our rider, an American Indian boy who had just been discharged from the service, briefly described his life to us. Then my companion began to try to witness to him. I sat, very quietly, watching the whole thing. That witness was absolutely leaden. There was no life in it, although all the doctrine that the young believer could muster was scripturally correct. For about forty-five minutes, his words were just falling to the ground.

Finally, our passenger had to get off. As we drove on, my friend's face was a picture of disillusionment. He was horribly disappointed and could not understand what had gone wrong. I sat there with my arms folded over my chest, gazing out of the window, just kind of whistling as if I were unaware of what was taking place. He was growing increasingly irritated, and I could sense the question burning in his soul: "Come on Katz, how about it, aren't you going to explain?"

I finally turned to him and said, "You did a very good thing to pick up a hitchhiker, very humane, very well-intending; but did it ever occur to you that a quarter of a mile up the road, there may have been another hitchhiker waiting, he whom God had intended for you to pick up in a divine encounter? But you had to pass him right by because the seat which God had intended for him to fill *you* have filled with your own good intentions."

169

By engaging in an activity which was humanly "good," he was disqualifying himself from the thing which was divinely perfect. The world is troubled by the choice between what *it* calls "good" and what *it* calls "evil." For the believer, the choice will more often be between the ostensibly good thing of men and the perfect thing of God. Our tendency and our temptation is always to do that "good" thing; we even want to "do good for the Lord."

Young people in particular are susceptible to this snare. The pressure is on. I see the phenomenon especially in *Jewish* young believers. They are told that they are no longer Jews, that they have copped out, that they are traitors, that they have forsaken their ancestral faith, and so on. They so often feel that they have to *do*, to perform, to somehow prove themselves, to show themselves strong in the Lord and favored by God. "Look how Jewish we are, look what we've done."

I cannot think of a more sickly spiritual tangle in this moment than Israel. Dozens of self-appointed ministers have gone to Israel like knights in shining armor to deliver the people and to show them the way to the Messiah. They are walking into walls and walking into each other. It's a welter of so-called "good" ministries which too often impede the true work of God.

God is working something in the earth of unspeakable magnitude and complexity today: there has never been an hour when the people of the Lord have needed to be more perfectly orchestrated in His purposes than now. Every clever product of our skulls and all our human intentions shall not only fall short of God's perfect plan, but will, whether we know it or not, oppose it.

Sabbath: The Perfect Rest of God

If you have read *Ben Israel*, you should know that if there

170

is anyone who should have a respect for picking up hitchhikers, it's Art Katz. My life in God began in Switzerland when a man picked me up in Winterthur and began to unfold to me the words of life. Yet, I myself do not *compulsively* pick up hitchhikers.

It is only recently that I feel myself coming into a freedom from all kinds of compulsive acting, from the pressure to perform, to do my thing, to show myself approved before God and men. I have been entering into the *Shabbat*, the *Shabbos:* the Sabbath rest of God. Hallelujah! It is a glory to come into this beautiful rest and to cease from your own labors.

I have often wondered why Jesus performed so many of His works on the *Shabbat*, upsetting all those Pharisees. Why couldn't He have waited until Sunday or Monday or Tuesday? He had six days to do His great miracles, but He seemed to intently go out of His way to do them on the Sabbath, although the Scriptures expressly forbid any man to work on that day. Why did Jesus exacerbate those Jewish men and rub salt into their wounds? He tried to explain to them but they could not understand.

It was only after ten years as a believer that I began to understand it myself. I have had many conversations with my Jewish people in which I have told them, "I have come into a new covenant. I didn't change religions. I'm still a Jew, *more* the Jew, and the same God who gave the old covenant gave a better one into which I've come. The law is written on my inward heart; it's no longer an outward manner, but an inward thing." Their next question would often be, "Well, are you keeping the Sabbath?" They might even quote the *Torah* (Pentateuch):

Wherefore the children of Israel shall keep the sabbath, to observe the sabbath throughout their

171

generations, for a perpetual covenant.

Exodus 31:16

I would then choke and splutter, "We don't have to fulfill the law in that way, we don't have to do, we're under grace. . . ," but I was never happy with my answer, and neither were they. In some subtle way, the question was being shoved aside, and the preciousness and beauty of the *Shabbat* was being denigrated.

To appreciate the importance of this whole question, you must know something of the part that the Sabbath has played in the history of my people. You must sample some of its flavor. There is a saying in Jewish life, "More than the Jews have kept the Sabbath, the Sabbath has kept the Jews." However much we have been an object of scorn, derision, persecution, and oppression, however much we have been forced to live in ghettos, little islands of Jews in seas of Gentile hostility, the *Shabbos* has kept us, has sustained us. We would look forward to its coming in anticipation of its joy.

The best of the dishes, the best clothing, the best of the food, the best of everything is kept for the *Shabbos*. The kids are scrubbed on that day until their faces are shining. During the rest of the week, you sweat, groan, and face bitter things in the world, but on Friday evening, you come into your own home, close the door, and rest. Wonderful smells emanate from the kitchen—chicken soup (Jewish penicillin), matzoh balls, all kinds of delightful goodies. Mother has cleansed the house and purged it from all *chummitz* (leaven). However poor a Jew is (oh yes, there *are* poor Jews), however threadbare the tablecloth is, it is washed clean, starched, perfectly ironed, and the finest of whatever is available is spread out upon it.

As the sun begins to set, ending the day and the week, the

mother lights the traditional Sabbath candles. After ceremonially motioning with her hands above the flames, she would then put her head in her hands, bow, and pray in Hebrew.

I cannot help but think of how this pattern relates to other times that God has delighted in using a woman at the inception of something holy in His sight. She has prepared and now she brings in the light, just as God brought the Light into the world through the Jewish woman, Mary. Recall also how the Lord chose to begin the Body of Christ in Macedonia and in all of the western world with the Philippian woman, Lydia.

Then the father, the priest of the home, takes over, lifting the wine cup, and reciting or singing the traditional Hebrew prayer, *"Baruch atah Adonai Elohenu Melech haolam boray p'ri hagofen."* ("Blessed art Thou, O Lord our God, King of the universe, Who createst the fruit of the vine.") With a sip from that cup, the Sabbath has officially begun. On Saturday at dusk, at the end of the Sabbath, there is a ceremony that fills the whole house with rich fragrances of spices. The joy of that day is so uplifting that even as you go into the week—Sunday, Monday, Tuesday, Wednesday—the memory of it is able to keep you. As you press more deeply into the week, the anticipation of the soon-returning Sabbath is enough to bring you again to a sustaining experience.

It is true that most Jews today have lost this sense of the beauty of the Sabbath and usually ignore it altogether, but to those who still cherish it I am now prepared to give answer: "Yes, I *am* keeping the Sabbath. Under the old covenant, you enjoy the *Shabbos* one day a week, and I know what a *mitzvah* (blessing) it is, but under the new covenant, which is a more perfect one, I am enjoying it *every day of the week."*

173

Truly, the Sabbath of my Jewish people (and of nominal Christendom) is *good*, but the rest of God in the hearts in which the Holy Spirit lives and over which He has dominion is *perfect*. There is no striving, no sweat, and the sweet fragrance is perpetual. Jesus said to His disciple Philip, ". . . the Father that dwelleth in me, he doeth the works" (John 14:10b). To His chagrined detractors the Lord spoke the same message:

> And therefore did the Jews persecute Jesus, and sought to slay him, because he had done these things on the sabbath day.
> But Jesus answered them, My Father worketh hitherto, and I work.
> Therefore the Jews sought the more to kill him, because he not only had broken the sabbath, but said also that God was his Father, making himself equal with God.
> Then answered Jesus and said unto them, Verily, verily, I say unto you, The Son can do nothing of himself, but what he seeth the Father do: for what things soever he doeth, these also doeth the Son likewise.
>
> John 5:16-19

If our lives are truly not our own, we too can affirm to a jeering world, "It is my Father who doeth the works." We need not worry about what condition we are in at any given time. It was totally inconsequential that, at the inception of those eight days of university gospel meetings, I knew that I was unable to answer that wise guy's intimidating question out of my own wisdom and experience: it is my Father who doeth the works. He is perfect. He is the Almighty.

I am not coming down upon setting aside one day unto the

Lord each week as a special day of rest; in our community in Minnesota, one day is, in fact, designated as a time of ceasing from our outward labors. One might call it our visible Sabbath; but there is an even more important rest, an invisible one, available to each of us *daily* as we seek to walk perfectly before our God, presenting our lives to Him as a living sacrifice. When the Spirit of the Lord directs our steps, our steps are perfect, and our hearts are at rest, for we know that we are living unto Him:

> One man esteemeth one day above another: another esteemeth every day alike. Let every man be fully persuaded in his own mind.
> He that regardeth the day, regardeth it *unto the Lord;* and he that regardeth not the day, *to the Lord* he doth not regard it.
>
> Romans 14:5, 6a
(our italics)

Two Trees

The rest of God is inseparable from the presence of His life. Watchman Nee, in a booklet called *Two Principles of Conduct*, writes,

> One of the most serious misconceptions among the children of God is that actions are determined by right and wrong. They do what their eyes tell them is right; they do what their background tells them is right; they do what their years of experience tells them is right. For a Christian, every decision should be based on the inner life, and that is something totally different from all else.[8]

Nee, in illustration of this truth, refers us to the two trees in

175

the midst of Eden's garden and to God's commandment concerning them:

> And out of the ground made the Lord God to grow every tree that is pleasant to the sight, and good for food; the tree of life also in the midst of the garden, and the tree of knowledge of good and evil.
> And the Lord God commanded the man, saying, Of every tree of the garden thou mayest freely eat:
> But of the tree of the knowledge of good and evil, thou shalt not eat of it: for in the day that thou eatest thereof thou shalt surely die.
>
> Genesis 2:9,16,17

As we all know, Adam and Eve did eat from that tree, poisoning the entire human race, and mankind has been eating from it ever since. The greater pity is that most believers are still eating from it, trusting in their human judgments, reason, exercise, will, striving, and exertion. They are living from the knowledge, not just of evil, but of good *and* evil. It is a cursed tree, a tree of death.

You say, "Katz, if we are not supposed to make our judgments on the basis of what we think is right or wrong or what our eyes, background or experience tell us, then on what basis do we live?" We live, not from the principle of the tree of the knowledge of good and evil, but from the principle of the tree of life. We live from the life of God. Jesus says, "I am the way, the truth, and the *life* . . ." (John 14:6a). There is no life apart from God's Son:

> He that believeth on the Son of God hath the witness in himself: he that believeth not God hath

made him a liar; because he believeth not the record that God gave of his Son.

And this is the record, that God hath given to us eternal life, and *this life is in his Son.*

He that hath the Son hath life; and he that hath not the Son of God hath not life.

1 John 5:10-12
(our italics)

When we depend upon the strength of our own flesh in the governance of our daily lives, we deprive ourselves of the fulness of God's gift of love to us. John writes in the previous chapter of the same letter:

> In this was manifested the love of God toward us, because that God sent his only begotten Son into the world, that we might *live* through him.

1 John 4:9
(our italics)

I once attended a Hebrew-Christian conference, and before long, I had a pain in my head, because much of what was going forth was cerebral, mental. It had its origin, not in the Spirit, but in the flesh. It was well-meaning, full of good intention, but it was human and not divine; it was not perfect, because it did not come from the heart of God. When I expressed my dissatisfaction to some of the leaders of the conference, they asked me what I thought of one of the principal speakers, adding, "He's like you. He's a Spirit-filled believer—speaks with tongues—just like you. Surely you can't have this complaint with him?"

Something started taking shape in my heart. I asked, "Then how come he uses all of these clever little tactics, and is so full of all of these goodies; cute little quips and jokes and endless little *schticklach* (affected mannerisms) and devices

177

to get the audience's attention?"

"Oh well," they said, "he's nervous, Art. He's insecure. He feels that if he doesn't use these things, he couldn't hold anyone's attention."

Suddenly the light of truth broke upon me. He may be "charismatic," he may be filled with the Holy Spirit and may speak with tongues, but, *in the moment of confrontation*, he abandoned all things that spring from God's life, and went back to the tree of the knowledge of good and evil. He was working out of his skull, out of his flesh, out of his human striving and energy; he was nervous and apprehensive because *he was not trusting the Lord*, not living by faith. "The just shall *live* by faith" (Romans 1:17b). Without faith, it is impossible to receive anything from God, and we have no faith if we do not truly rest in God's very life within us, knowing that our old man has gone with Jesus to the cross:

> I am crucified with Christ: nevertheless I live; yet not I, but Christ liveth in me: and the life which I now live in the flesh *I live by the faith of the Son of God*, who loved me, and gave himself for me.
>
> Galatians 2:20
> (our italics)

At any given moment, a moment of witness, a moment of ministry, a moment of relationship, a moment of any kind of religious activity or service, we can refuse to live through God and choose to live from ourselves. In any moment of our own choosing, we can abandon Him and trust in our own devices. In that moment, we have left the perfect and have adopted only the "good." The alternatives before us are either the unfolding of the glories of God in our lives or a whole lot of coming and going, having and spending, sweating, striving, grinding, and exertion. All of that activity, though it be done in the holy name of the Lord, will, if its origin is not in Him, have no capacity to bring life, because He alone *is* the life.

Above and Below

Every good gift and every perfect gift is from above, and cometh down from the Father of lights, with whom is no variableness, neither shadow of turning.

James 1:17

There is no more perfect gift that comes to us from above than the rest of God, issuing forth from His very life. To turn from a total, childlike dependency upon the Holy Spirit is to choose death in all of its forms and to relinquish the Sabbath covenant. The writer to the Hebrews, quoting from the ninety-fifth Psalm, clearly presents the grave consequences of Israel's unbelief:

Wherefore (as the Holy Ghost saith, Today if ye will hear his voice,

Harden not your hearts, as in the provocation, in the day of temptation in the wilderness:

When your fathers tempted me, proved me, and saw my works forty years.

Wherefore I was grieved with that generation, and said, They do always err in their heart; and they have not known my ways.

So I sware in my wrath, They shall not enter into my rest.)

Hebrews 3:7-11

Of all the consequences that they might have suffered, God singled out one; He made one statement, and it says everything: "They shall not enter into my rest." There is the suggestion here that God has reserved something so unspeakably holy, so sacred, that it is the ultimate dimension of experience for the people of God, and Israel missed it.

God, from the depths of His loving heart, is exhorting us to cleave wholly to His life within us and to utterly reject the serpentine appeals from below which would encourage us to a proud independence. Believing on Christ, cleaving wholly to Him, is the key:

> And to whom sware he that they should not enter into his rest, but to them that believed not?
> So we see that they could not enter in because of unbelief.
> Let us therefore fear, lest, a promise being left us of entering into his rest, any of you should seem to come short of it.
>
> Hebrews 3:18,19; 4:1

Do we, in fact, have this holy fear of coming short of God's perfect rest? Is there anything more sweaty than American evangelism? Cranking out tens upon tens of thousands of tracts, laboriously coming and going, screaming from bull horns, knocking on doors, are we moving in and for the Lord, or are we just running around in the nervous little circles of our own restless unbelief? We think that our service for God is measured by the quantity of activity we are involved with, or with the volume of noise that we make. The same mentality seems to afflict our services. The truth is that it is in the silence that we are more likely to find God.

We Americans seem to be afraid of the quiet. This generation has grown up with transistor radios glued to its heads, unable even to do its homework without the television, radio, or record player going. Many of us are not quite sure that we are alive unless we have something to fill the spaces or some activity to busy ourselves with. The author of confusion, who loves to try to turn God's truth inside out and upside down, has many of the Lord's children fully distracted by the clatter and rush of this world, but God affirms:

> There remaineth therefore a rest to the people of God.
> For he that is entered into his rest, he also hath ceased from his own works, as God did from his.
> Hebrews 4:9,10

We are then presented with a paradox:

> *Let us labour therefore to enter into that rest,* lest any man fall after the same example of unbelief.
> Hebrews 4:11

The truth of our God is always paradoxical, for it contradicts every expectation of the carnal mind. Look at how the Lord had to deal with Peter, for example. That disciple is the perfect picture of a certain variety of modern Christian: gung ho, wanting to "do" for God, well-meaning, a hot shot ready to take the world, who is quick to say,

> Though all men shall be offended because of thee, yet will I never be offended. . . . Though I should

die with thee, yet will I not deny thee. . . . Lord, I am ready to go with thee, both into prison, and to death.

Matthew 26:33, 35
Luke 22:33

The Lord, who knows all men's hearts, knew, of course, that Peter would deny Him three times before the crowing of the cock. That is why He had to say to him, ". . . when thou art converted, strengthen thy brethren" (Luke 22:32b). Many who have answered altar calls have never actually been converted. They are still living by their own strength, their own strivings, and have not been *wholly turned around* from the tree of the knowledge of good and evil to the tree of life. "When you are converted, when you are no longer living out of your own pompous assertions, thinking you are going to take the world by your strength, *then* go and strengthen your brethren. When you are emptied out, *then* go strengthen." Isn't that a paradoxical God?

What was required of Peter is required of us also: an emptying out of self, that God might be all in all in our lives. Remember Jacob, the supplanter, the schemer, the wheeler-dealer, striving to do his own thing and getting into all kinds of hot water. Separated from his family and from all of his possessions, he was emptied out and left alone with God at the ford Jabbok:

> And Jacob was left alone; and there wrestled a man with him until the breaking of the day.
> And when he saw that he prevailed not against him, he touched the hollow of his thigh; and the hollow of Jacob's thigh was out of joint, as he wrestled with him.

And he said, Let me go, for the day breaketh. And he said, I will not let thee go, except thou bless me.

And he said unto him, What is thy name? And he said, Jacob.

And he said, Thy name shall be called no more Jacob, but Israel: for as a prince hast thou power with God and with men, and hast prevailed.

And Jacob asked him, and said, Tell me, I pray thee, thy name. And he said, Wherefore is it that thou dost ask after my name? And he blessed him there.

And Jacob called the name of the place Peniel: for I have seen God face to face, and my life is preserved.

And as he passed over Penuel the sun rose upon him, and he halted upon his thigh.

Genesis 32:24-31

Every man, every self-assertive Jacob, who has had an encounter with the living God, wrestling with Him and being brought to the end of his own desperate devices and attempts (however well-meaning) to obtain the blessing, shall be touched "in the hollow of the thigh." There will be a lameness, not necessarily of the body, but in the human spirit. After the touch of God, we find ourselves limping where we had formerly dashed with proud self-assurance. What does being touched in the hollow of the thigh bespeak? That is where we men live; our virility, our sexual prowess, is located there. It is in the hollows, in the joints, in the marrow of our bones, that our blood is manufactured. It is the seat of our life, our strength, our self-sufficiency, and that is exactly where God has got to put His finger to make us lame—that is, completely dependent upon Him.

Emptied out, we can receive the fulness of the Almighty, that we might be His princes, having power with God and with men. Repeatedly, God's word presents us with this truth:

> . . . the lame take the prey. . . . Not by might, nor by power, but by my spirit, saith the Lord of hosts.
>
> Isaiah 33:23b
> Zechariah 4:6b

The Lord said to Paul, after the apostle had besought Him three times to remove his humbling infirmity, his "thorn in the flesh,"

> . . . My grace is sufficient for thee: for my strength is made perfect in weakness.
>
> 2 Corinthians 12:9a

Paul's response gives us a clear presentation of the divine paradox:

> Most gladly therefore will I rather glory in my infirmities, that the power of Christ may rest upon me.
>
> Therefore I take pleasure in infirmities, in reproaches, in necessities, in persecutions, in distresses for Christ's sake: for when I am weak, then am I strong.
>
> 2 Corinthians 12:9b, 10

Without the acknowledgment of our fundamental

weakness and of the Lord's all-sufficient strength, we shall never enter into the perfect rest of God's children. It is a serious deception, inspired by the enemy of our souls, to believe that we can ever attain to perfection and spiritual peace without having the Spirit of Jesus dwelling and working within us. Who is this Jesus?

> When Jesus came into the coasts of Caesarea Philippi, he asked his disciples, saying, Whom do men say that I the Son of man am?
>
> Matthew 16:13

There is no question of greater importance for our generation than that one. Satan is quite busy in this hour, as he was in the day of the first disciples, trying to answer it in his own way:

> And they said, Some say that thou art John the Baptist: some, Elias; and others, Jeremias, or one of the prophets.
>
> Matthew 16:14

The world, which lies in the power of the evil one, has no lack of answers to the Lord's question, all of which are diabolically designed to degrade His true image: "You are the inspiration for tee-shirts, jewelry, and rock musicals." Like their predecessors, they might even grant, in apparent magnanimity, "You are one of the great teachers and prophets." If we chose to, we could compile a very lengthy catalogue of who men say that the Son of Man is, but we would be sidetracking the central issue in our own life: "He saith unto them, But whom say ye that I am?" (Matthew 16:15) How I love that about the Lord: not content to raise that profound question abstractly, He puts His finger right on our chest, and says, "Who do YOU say that I am?"

That question is never answered once and for all by any one of us; by His Spirit guiding us into all truth, we come to a progressive and increasing knowledge of who He is. We should never rest content, thinking that we know Him as we ought. We are only at the beginning.

> And ye shall seek me, and find me, when ye shall
> search for me with all your heart.
> And I will be found of you, saith the Lord. . . .
> Jeremiah 29:13,14a

As a young believer, I used to read that passage and think that in salvation I had arrived at the ultimate knowledge of Him; but, then as now, I was only at the beginning, scratching the surface of the infinite God. We shall continue to seek and continue to be found of God, and shall never come to the end of His glories.

Who is the first one to answer the Lord's question? Mr. Self-confidence himself:

> And Simon Peter answered and said, Thou art
> the Christ, the Son of the living God.
> Matthew 16:16

I would not be surprised if Peter threw his chest out at this point, for the answer that he gave was true. Often, we think that because we have given the right answer, we have arrived; we can demand an "A" for the day and go to the head of the class. God is the source of all truth, and, by the Spirit, leads us into it. It is our pride that imagines that our carnal minds can ever be the origin of divine revelation. The Lord is quick to point this out:

> And Jesus answered and said unto him, Blessed
> art thou, Simon Bar-jona: for flesh and blood hath
> not revealed it unto thee, but my Father which is
> in heaven.
>
> Matthew 16:17

This correct identification is the beginning of blessing.
The Scriptures clearly give us two alternatives for every
life—blessing or curse. Anyone who has not come to this
initial blessing in the identification of who Jesus is, be he Jew
or Gentile, is living under a curse, separated from the
Father. The Lord requires of us, however, more than this
first step. There are countless "Christian" religionists who
do not know as they ought to know who Jesus is, though they
can glibly say, "the Messiah, the Son of the Living God." For
Jesus truly to become our Messiah, He had to choose the one
perfect path ordained by the Father:

> From that time forth began Jesus to shew unto
> his disciples, how that he must go unto Jerusalem,
> and suffer many things of the elders and chief
> priests and scribes, and be killed, and be raised
> again the third day.
>
> Matthew 16:21

As we saw in our consideration of these verses at the end
of the first chapter, the mission of our Lord Jesus upon this
earth is inseparable from the cross. Like Peter, we are quick
to give answer to the first question, proclaiming Jesus as
Christ, but we are not as quick to receive the truth of what
must follow: the inevitability of suffering and death.

> Then Peter took him, and began to rebuke him,
> saying, Be it far from thee, Lord: this shall not be
> unto thee.
>
> Matthew 16:22

Today, the speaker of such a statement could win a Nobel prize, or at least an honorary doctorate from many universities in the world. It is full of right intention and noble concern, the epitome of all that the world applauds as humane, considerate, and kind; but what did Jesus say of it?

> But he turned, and said unto Peter, Get thee
> behind me, Satan: thou art an offence unto me: for
> thou savourest not the things that be of God, but
> those that be of men.
>
> Matthew 16:23

None of us have pondered this response of Jesus as deeply as we ought to. Many who go by the Lord's name have not yet terminated their flirtation with the world, and are still enamored of its universities, its honors, its blandishments, its rewards, and its ethics. There exists the belief that we can somehow make a happy medley of things sacred and things human, with everything lumped together under the banner of "the good."

Jesus seemed to have a much simpler view of the entire situation. *He saw things coming from only two places: above and below.* Things that are divine and perfect come down from the Father of lights: everything which does not have its origin in Him springs from the underworld. "Get thee behind me, Satan: you are an offense to me: you do not savor the things that are of God, but *those that are of men.* You are quoting from the tree of the knowledge of good and evil and

188

not from the tree of life. All of your righteousnesses are as filthy rags. They are an offense to me."

Certainly what Peter suggested was a "good" thing. Jesus, however, rejected the thing which is "good," calling it satanic, and insisted upon the thing which is perfect, the thing which is divine. He suffered and died for the salvation of mankind.

To allow the "good" to displace the perfect is to succumb to the tempting voices which rise from the pit, crying, "Be it far from thee." To choose God's perfect way is to say yes to the inevitability of suffering and death, trusting that the holy life of Christ Himself filling us will be the sure consequence of our decision.

> Then said Jesus unto his disciples, If any man will come after me, let him deny himself, and take up his cross, and follow me.
> For whosoever will save his life shall lose it: and whosoever will lose his life for my sake shall find it.
> Matthew 16:24,25

Actively Resting

Years ago, in Kansas City, I spoke at a huge Presbyterian Church which was tentatively reaching out for the first time to the Jewish community. The committee that had arranged it was trembling. This was not only the first time that they had ever extended this kind of invitation to Jews; it was the first time that *any* kind of evangelistic meeting had been held in that building. Before the beginning of the service, there was a banquet where they served ham topped with chicken slices! A man who operated a Cadillac agency came up to me there, and said, "Mr. Katz, are you going to give one of those Billy Graham type invitations when this is over?"

189

"I usually do," I answered. "I'll almost never speak without inviting men to call upon the name of the Lord."

"Well, what happens if some people respond, and, as you say, get saved? Isn't it all over then, finished? Where do you go from there? I mean, *then* what?"

"Dear brother," I said, "the book that follows the Gospels is the Book of ACTS."

God is not calling us to passivity and inaction; He is calling us to *cease from our own labors*, that we might enter into His rest, as His perfect works are done in our lives, for His purpose, and for His eternal glory. May God keep us from impeding any of those holy tasks. May we not forget that it is *"in Him"* that "we live, and move, and have our being." (Acts 17:28a) We in Him and He in us: this is the key that opens the paradoxes and mysteries of God to us. Paul wrote to the church at Philippi:

> . . . work out your own salvation with fear and trembling.
> For it is God which worketh in you both to will and to do of his good pleasure.
>
> Philippians 2:12b,13

I love the way the same wonderful paradox of grace reads in the Amplified Version:

> . . . work out—cultivate, carry out to the goal and fully complete—your own salvation with reverence and awe and trembling [self-distrust, that is, with serious caution, tenderness of conscience, watchfulness against temptation; timidly shrinking from whatever might offend God and discredit the name of Christ].

> [Not in your own strength] for it is God Who is
> all the while effectually at work in
> you—energizing and creating in you the power
> and desire—both to will and to work for His good
> pleasure and satisfaction and delight.

To labor to enter into God's rest is to seek only His good pleasure as the fruit of your life, not your own; with hearts that are possessed by the Lord, we can act with assurance that the Holy Spirit shall empower and enable us for the carrying out of the Father's will.

Though the schedules of our activities and commitments may get increasingly demanding (which has been the case with my own schedule), we need not be harried and restless in our souls, as long as we live from the life of the Almighty God. There was a time when, at the end of a month of meetings, I would feel exhausted, spent, and useless for any further service—in a word, *finished*. Now, in months which are even more demanding and packed with the most consequential works of God, I generally am as fresh on the last day as I was on the first. To the extent that I reject living from my own strength or wisdom, and live from the faith of the Son of God, to that same extent do I taste of God's sacred rest.

Too often, we who go by the Lord's name underestimate the riches of the inheritance we have in Him "in whom are hid *all* the treasures of wisdom and knowledge" (Colossians 2:3). That brief verse in Paul's letter to the Colossian Church is a sister statement to Genesis 17:1: "I am the Almighty God; walk before me, and be thou perfect." We should all take a pen to Colossians 2:3 and heavily underscore the word *all*. "All" is not merely the name of a laundry detergent. The English language has suffered terrible abuse in our generation; in fact, every standard is falling.

We are entering the time in which God's description of the sinful Israel of the seventh century B.C. is applicable also to this present world:

> And judgment is turned away backward, and justice standeth afar off: for truth is fallen in the street, and equity cannot enter.
>
> Isaiah 59:14

Even the lesser human standards that have given us some kind of semblance of civilization and decency shall come tumbling down; men shall move like packs of animals, pillaging, raping, and murdering, in the streets of our great cities. In that spreading darkness and gloom, God shall shine forth His glorious perfection through us. The world will stand before us with the kind of amazement that stunned me as I beheld that linen closet in Jerusalem, as they see the splendor of God's perfect order in our lives. We shall not be applauded for our conspicuous differences, but shall receive the response from the world that I received from that Jewish woman in the high school cafeteria in Oakland: "Art, even when you're silent, you're a living accusation!"

> So shall they fear the name of the Lord from the west, and his glory from the rising of the sun. When the enemy shall come in like a flood, the Spirit of the Lord shall lift up a standard against him.
>
> Isaiah 59:19

That holy standard shall rise *in us*, as we, in faith, act in childlike reliance upon the Spirit of the Almighty God, resting assured that *in Him* are hidden ALL the treasures of wisdom and knowledge.

Crowns of Thorns and Glory

> Know ye not, that so many of us as were baptized into Jesus Christ were baptized into his death?
>
> Therefore we are buried with him by baptism into death: that like as Christ was raised up from the dead by the glory of the Father, even so we also should walk in newness of life.
>
> Romans 6:3,4

After I was baptized, I used to kid my pastor and say, "Why didn't you keep me under longer?" I had wanted to consciously tick off all of the aspects of the old Art Katz life (of course, had he kept me under long enough to do *that*, there would have been a death indeed). The waters of baptism are God's judgment on all flesh. How needful it was for this Jewish head, crammed with all sorts of knowledge, to be submerged, covered by those waters, that I might say with Paul, "For I determined not to know anything among you, save Jesus Christ, and him crucified" (1 Corinthians 2:2). I am determined to have this mind crucified, buried, and hidden. It shall not run my life, but I shall run it by the Spirit of God; it is only a handmaiden, not made to dominate or possess.

The beginning of the third chapter of Colossians speaks to those who have joined our Messiah in death, burial, and resurrection:

> If ye then be risen with Christ, seek those things which are above, where Christ sitteth on the right hand of God.
>
> Set your affection on things above, not on things on the earth.
>
> Colossians 3:1,2

193

Again, the Lord whittles away all of our categories until just two are left: above and below. Choosing those things which are above is the only alternative consistent with being a baptized believer; it is choosing life, blessing, light, faith, and rest, and rejecting death, cursing, darkness, doubt, and all the mad restlessness of human effort.

> For ye are dead, and your life is hid with Christ in God.
> When Christ, who is our life, shall appear, then shall ye also appear with him in glory.
>
> Colossians 3:3,4

We have seen how the examples of Joseph, Elijah, and Paul and Silas stand in stark contrast to the frenetic glory seeking of worldly men both within and without Christendom. Those Jewish men sought, above all things, to be in the perfect will of their Lord, and were content with obscurity, humiliation and suffering. At the bottom of a pit, at a dried brook, backs hanging in bloody shreds in a Philippian jail, they waited for the revelation of God's glory.

Unless we too are willing to accept that first part, to be dead to this world and have our lives hidden with Christ in God, His glory shall not be revealed in us. There can be no receiving of the crown of glory without, first, the willingness to wear the crown of thorns. This was the way of Jesus and it must be our way also.

> Herein is our love made perfect, that we may have boldness in the day of judgment: because as he is, so are we in this world.
>
> 1 John 4:17

We cannot foreknow every detail of the outworking of

God's perfect purpose. Our readiness to engage in critical spiritual confrontations is not to be contingent upon our knowledge of their outcome, but only upon the fact of God's having called us there. Whether thorns or glory await us in any given situation the Lord knows. To rest in Him, trusting in His perfect wisdom and love, is the sole requirement and the holy privilege given to the servants of the Lord.

> O the depth of the riches both of the wisdom and knowledge of God! how unsearchable are his judgments, and his ways past finding out!
> For who hath known the mind of the Lord? or who hath been his counsellor?
>
> Romans 11:33,34

A few years ago on a Friday night, I came to Harvard University, whacked out of my skull with exhaustion. It had been a fast day. I used to fast regularly on particular days of the week, and especially on days when there was to be prominent ministry. I cannot honestly say that I had entered fully into God's rest, but I was beginning to have a partial understanding of it. By evening, I was so out of it that I could hardly remember my name; hungry, wasted, tired, dull, a mouth like sawdust, hot, sweaty, gritty, I was a first-class mess. I hoped that the audience would be very small so that I could escape with a minimum of embarrassment.

To my amazement, when I entered the room, it was jammed to the rafters. There must have been three hundred students and it was a coliseum atmosphere. "Where is this Jewish freak who believes in Jesus? Let us at him—boy, what fun!" That was the spirit. Thinking about their reputation, I took one look at that assembly, and my heart sank. I could only hope that the floor would open up and swallow me. I thought, "Lord, you've bailed me out of many

195

situations before, but this is one that's even going to tax your power."

I took my jacket off and threw it on a table in semi-resignation to my fate, like a man going to the guillotine, ready to be blindfolded. I said to those students, "I had hoped tonight to prepare something clever, knowing your reputation, but my condition is such that you're going to have only one of two alternatives. You're going to see a pitiful human fiasco, or you're going to see the glory of God."

How would you like *that* to be your standard operating procedure, your only alternatives in every occasion in which you are called to the service of God? Human fiasco or God's glory. Many of us would rather not have either of those alternatives intruding upon our private little plans. Is there a way to escape tasting of the mortification, suffering, and death or of the glory? Not if you are going to walk in the Way, not if you choose to be perfect and walk before Him.

God knows how to temper His saints and sees to it that we do not have too many consecutive glories, lest we become exalted in our own eyes. We go from glory to mortification and vice versa in that breath-like rhythm of pits and peaks which marked the lives of Joseph, Elijah, Paul, and every saint who has learned in the school of the Spirit that *all* glory belongs to God.

I opened my mouth in that Harvard room, fully expecting the worst, and, out of my pitiful weakness, to my own astonishment, came a blast of God, straight from His heart. It was such a thoroughly penetrating and incisive dissertation on the human condition that not one man in that room could find a place to hide. The power of the Spirit stopped every mouth and riveted men to their seats. They looked like people on a jet plane, pinned back by the thrust of a takeoff. For the first time in my university speaking experience, not one wise guy stood up to bait me with quips, wisecracks, and malicious questions. The same men who had come to jeer and to make sport sat in stunned silence; they knew that God was in their midst and was speaking to them. It is the Father who doeth the works.

I was so stunned that I did not know what to do next. There was nothing more to be said except, "You know, Jesus said, 'My sheep hear my voice, and I know them, and they follow me: And I give unto them eternal life . . .' (John 10: 27,28a). I invite as many of you who have heard His voice out of this Brooklyn accent to follow me in a prayer for your salvation." I bowed my head, recited a sinner's prayer, and, to my amazement, heard a chorus of what must have been well over a hundred voices. The glory of God had so filled that room that my hair was standing up on my arms. In that holy hush, I lifted my head and saw weeping, trembling, shaking, giggling, all of the varieties of responses of men to whom the Holy Spirit has just come. Where does one go from there? I could only say, "Let us raise our hands before Him and praise the God who has just saved us." At Harvard University, that citadel of self-glorification, student rebellion, and death in all of its forms, men who had come to ridicule and blaspheme had their hands above their heads praising God.

God had visited that campus, heaping glory upon glory. Demonic spirits were cast out. The Christian students who had invited me were on their faces before God, making a new commitment in a depth and consecration that they had not previously known was available. A woman from the community came up to me after the meeting and said, "Would you pray me a blessing?"

Feeling like an ancient Hebrew patriarch, I said, "What blessing do you want?"

Without a moment's hesitation, she said, "The Holy Spirit."

About fifteen stunned students, many of them Jewish, stood around us, listening to that woman's request. I asked her, "Do you believe that when I put my hand on your forehead, God, who sees your thirsty heart, will fill it?" With full assurance of faith she said that she did. At the moment that I touched her head and just began to pray, that woman, who had never before spoken in tongues, broke forth in a stream of heavenly praise right in front of those secular students who had never seen nor heard such a supernatural phenomenon. God's strength was made perfect in my weakness and my nothingness, and we had a night in which His glory was revealed.

It would be unfair to end on this note without giving you the other side of the coin. We had another university meeting, at City College in New York, which, at that time, was eighty-five per cent Jewish. Months before, I had spoken to a Christian group there; God had come down by His Spirit and we wept because we knew that God was saying that we should have an outreach at that school.

What preparations we had for that meeting. We stinted at nothing, pouring out money, posters, and publicity; fasting and praying, we set up a chain of prayer bands all around the city. I was persuaded that *finally* God was going to do it. This was what we had been waiting for. Glory was going to break. The fire of God was going to fall. Jewish kids would fall on their faces in repentant tears, the sparks were going to be taken into their homes, and for the first time there was going to be an extensive penetration in the Jewish communities of New York City because of our obedience to God.

On the night before the meeting, I had spoken at Boston University, and then stayed up until four in the morning with my Jewish host, talking about the Lord. The thought came to me at one point, "Katz, you ought to get some rest." I countered with, "Oh no, I don't need it. Man, I've seen what God has done in my weakness. My condition is irrelevant. I know that the Lord is going to pour out great glories tomorrow. We've fasted, we've prayed, He's established this, we're in His will. I don't need rest." I stayed up talking.

On the next morning, I flew to New York City and was driven right from the airport to the meeting. When I arrived, a few minutes late, the room was packed and the atmosphere was so thick you could cut it with a knife. That audience was bristling with an electric hatred, bitterness, and hostility that could shrivel the most stalwart heart. If ever there was an encounter, this was it; yet I was supremely confident in God. The Lord had done it at Harvard. He could do it anywhere.

I came to the pulpit, breathed a little prayer, and began to speak. Right after the first word, I knew that I had had it—no anointing, no unction, nothing. It was the most pitiful, weak, beggarly dribble that I have ever heard. It just fell out of my mouth and onto the ground. I felt like a boxer who, after the first thirty seconds of the first round, knows he is beyond his class; if he can make it to the end of the fight without getting killed, he'll be happy.

There was nothing to do but to grit my teeth and finish. At the end of my pathetic little presentation, I opened, in my usual manner, for questions and answers. Among the many men wearing yarmulkes (head coverings) and sporting Vandyke beards was the rabbi from the Hillel Foundation, the Jewish student organization; he was the first one to stand up. Did that guy ever work me over. He told the audience what a fool, imbecile and ignoramus I am, that I don't speak Hebrew, that I came with medieval concepts to a modern university and tried to foist them upon an audience of intellectuals, that I was proclaiming the religion that had recently taken six million Jewish lives. I just stood there.

When he was finished, he stormed toward the exit, his heels clicking loudly on the floor. When he slammed the door, the whole room shook. I took a little gasp for air and another guy got up and continued where the rabbi had left off. One after another, in a seemingly endless chain, Jewish men stood to their feet and let me have it. By the time it was over, I was left for dead.

The worst was yet to come. It was hard to receive the ugly, cutting, bruising comments of my Jewish kinsmen, but it was immeasurably more painful to look into the disappointed faces of my Christian colleagues. They didn't say a word, but those countenances spoke volumes: "Katz, you've failed us. We thought it would have been YOU who would have restored the glory of Israel. We thought you were an anointed vessel of God. We thought you were experienced in these kinds of meetings. We staked everything on you, and you were pitiful. Don't you know how to fast and pray? Are you in sin?" I could not answer them a word, for God was not quick to give me so much as an iota of explanation.

I had come to that place seeking, like Elijah, the falling of fire from heaven. I had known that I was in God's perfect will, and my heart was filled with the prayer that that old prophet had cried out to God from the peak of Mount Carmel·

> And it came to pass at the time of the offering of the evening sacrifice, that Elijah the prophet came near, and said, Lord God of Abraham, Isaac, and of Israel, let it be known this day that thou art God in Israel, and that I am thy servant, and that I have done all these things at thy word.
>
> 1 Kings 18:36

At Harvard, I had expected a crown of thorns, but glory flooded the room. In the hour of reckoning at City College, fully expecting God's fire to fall, I walked into nothing but humiliation, defeat, and scorn: it was the crown of thorns. If we are unwilling to wear that crown, even unto death, we shall not enjoy fellowship with the despised and rejected Holy One of Israel. To reject the crown of thorns is to reject the crown of glory. As it is written, "Be thou faithful unto death, and I will give thee a crown of life" (Revelation 2:10b).

I went home that day with my tail between my legs, devastated, broken to pieces, smashed and ground to powder. I sulked and whimpered like a whipped dog, unable to rid my mind of the disappointed looks of my colleagues. I was in that condition, seriously sick in my soul, for three weeks, and then, one night, the phone rang.

A woman with a thin, little, raspy voice said almost inaudibly, "Mr. Katz, I'm a Jewish woman. I read your book. Can I come over and speak to you?" I thought, "Is there anybody who wants to speak to me? Is there anything that I can do for anybody, in my condition?" I said, "If you want to come, come."

She arrived shortly after, a woman so thin that she seemed almost transparent. A nervous wreck, a compulsive chain smoker, she appeared nigh unto death. She told me that, three weeks ago, her son, a City College student, had attended a meeting. He had come home speaking about a Jewish man who, after standing and simply setting forth his convictions, was attacked without mercy. What had so impressed him was that the man had just stood there without returning evil for evil. That Jewish boy had brought home a copy of *Ben Israel* and insisted that his mother read it. Now she had some questions for me.

After about an hour or two, after she had asked her last

question and snubbed out her last cigarette in the ash tray, she bowed her head and followed me in a prayer to call upon the name of the Lord. One little thin Jewish woman was saved out of death for time and eternity by the grace of our Messiah Jesus who would have died for her alone. Had the Lord not reserved a crown of thorns for me, that woman would not have been delivered from darkness that day. Again, Paul's words rang out clearly in my heart, "So then death worketh in us, but life in you" (2 Corinthians 4:12). How we can buck against the perfect work that God wishes to do in our lives by restlessly striving to find glory without thorns, resurrection without crucifixion, joy without sorrow, life without death.

Today that woman is a little missionary for God, running up and down the floors of her apartment house in Queens, witnessing and handing out tracts and literature. She has become a little Jewish dynamo in the modest context in which God has placed her, a source of life to others. Because of my unbelief, I had been cut off from God's wonderful rest for those three dark weeks; my gaze had fallen upon my own wretched natural condition and had drifted away from Jesus. To stop trusting in the heart, mind, and purposes of Christ is to open ourselves to the sorrow of this world. While I was lamenting my poor showing amongst my Christian brethren, the heart of my God was bursting with love for the languishing soul of that one "insignificant" woman, a Lydia hidden away from the spotlights of our public meeting places.

> For the Son of man is come to save that which was lost.
> How think ye? if a man have an hundred sheep, and seeketh that which is gone astray?
> And if so be that he find it, verily I say unto you,

he rejoiceth more of that sheep, than of the ninety and nine which went not astray.

Matthew 18:11-13

It was God's mercy and grace that He allowed me to see the salvation of that one soul. He is under no obligation to reveal to us the fruit that grows out of the soil of our humiliation, suffering, and death for His name's sake. It is enough for us to know that we are in the Messiah Jesus, the bleeding Lamb of God. He is the way, the truth, and the life, the first and the last, our all in all.

As ye have therefore received Christ Jesus the Lord, so walk ye *in him*:

Rooted and built up *in him*, and stablished in the faith, as ye have been taught, abounding therein with thanksgiving.

Beware lest any man spoil you through philosophy and vain deceit, after the tradition of men, after the rudiments of the world, and not after Christ.

For *in him* dwelleth all the fulness of the Godhead bodily.

And ye are *complete in him*, which is the head of all principality and power.

Colossians 2:6-10
(our italics)

Complete! There can be no such fulness outside of Christ. We are complete *in Him*. What will release that divine completeness, that perfect life, is our willingness to walk in the crucified way, to walk as Jesus walked before the Father. "I am the Almighty God; walk thou before me, and be thou perfect " Come to the cross. Dead to our own

203

intentions and strivings, resting in the perfect will of God, we can be content to be unseen, unheard, hidden, ignored, humiliated, mistreated, *whatever*, until it shall please Him to reveal His glory through us.

Notes

1. Elie Wiesel, *Night*, tr. Stella Rodway, Avon Books (Discus Edition), New York, 1969, p. 16.

2. *Ibid.*, p. 16

3. *Ibid.*, p. 18

4. *Ibid.*, p. 19

5. *Ibid.*, p. 31

6. *Ibid.*, p. 33

7. William Law, *The Power of the Spirit*, ed. Dave Hunt, Christian Literature Crusade, Pennsylvania, 1971, p.. 186-187.

8. Watchman Nee, *Two Principles of Conduct*, The Stream Publishers, Anaheim, California, pp. 11-12, used by permission.